second edition

Believing
and Experiencing

For WJEC specification B, Unit 2

Gavin Craigen
and Joy White

HODDER
EDUCATION
AN HACHETTE UK COMPANY

The Publishers would like to thank the following for permission to reproduce copyright material:

Photo credits

p.2 Courtesy Judy van Hoy; **p.14** *t* Getty Images/AFP/Patrick Baz, *b* Reuters/Kai Pfaffenbach; **p.16** PA Photos/David Cheskin; **p.17** *l* PA Photos/Carl Court, *r* PA Photos/Chiang Ying-ying; **p.20** Rex Features; **p.21** Tariq Khamisa Foundation; **p.22** The Corrymeela Community; **p.23** The Children of Abraham/photo of Uzma Ali 2004; **p.24** Peace One Day; **p.26** The Jewish Chronicle; **p.27** Associated Press/Elizabeth Dalziel; **p.28** Liverpool Youth Council; **p.31** PA Photos/Martin Rickett; **p.32** Ralph Singh, Gobind Sadan Gurdwara; **p.33** United Features Syndicate inc; **p.35** Culture and Sport Glasgow (Museums); **p.36** *t* Corbis/Angelo Hornak, *b* Corbis/Arthur Thevanart; **p.37** Tate Images; **p.39** *tl* & *tr* Corbis/David Turnley, *bl* Corbis/Roger Ressmeyer, *br* PA Photos/Adam Butler; **p.40** PA Photos/Ashwini Bhatia; **p.41** *tr* Topfoto/James Nubile/The Image Works, *l* PA Photos/Jerome Delay, *br* PA Photos/Hatem Moussa; **p.49** *The Independent,* text by Jeremy Laurance 26 March 2008; **p.54** European Press Agency/Paco Perez; **p.58** PA Photos/Martin Rickett; **p.61** News Team International Ltd; **p.70** *t* CAFOD, *b* CAFOD/Annie Bungeroth; **p.71** *l* & *r* Karuna Hospice Services; **p.72** SEWA/ Ahmedabad, India; **p.73** *l* & *r* Islamic Relief; **p.74** *l* Zigy Kaluzny, *r* Jewish Action & Training for Sexual Health; **p.75** Khalsa Aid; **p.79** *t* PA Photos/John Stillwell, *b* PA Photos/Barry Batchelor; **p.91** Alamy; **p.92** World Religions Photo Library/Christine Osborne; **p.93** James Davis Travel Photo Library; **p.94** Eye Ubiquitous/Hutchison/David Cumming; **p.95** Getty Images/George Hunter; **p.96** Alamy; **p.97** Getty Images/Gary Cralle; **p.98** Getty Images/AFP/Munish Sharma; **p.100** *tl* Getty Images/AFP/Lucy Nicholson, *bl* Corbis/James Leynse, *br* Christian Publicity Organisation; **p.118** Magnum Photos/ Steve McCurry; **p.126** *tl* Jude Spacks, *bl* PA Photos/Jeff Moore, *br* PA Photos/Andy Manis; **p.127** *l* Mary Evans Picture Library, *r* Corbis/SABA/Louise Gubb; **p.128** TopFoto/The Image Works; **p.135** Corbis/Flip Schulke.

Text acknowledgements

The Publishers would like to acknowledge use of the following extracts:

p.7 'It isn't right to fight', c. 1995 John Foster from 'Standing on the Sidelines' (Oxford University Press), included by permission of the author; **p.53** Extract adapted from the *Daily Mail*, 29 December 2006; **p.56** Extract adapted from *The Times*, 17 October 2008; **p.60** Extract from the *Daily Mail*, 24 September 2007; **p.79** *t* Extract adapted from the *Guardian*, 15 October 2006 *b* Extract from *Eastern Eye*, August 2008.

Every effort has been made to trace all copyright holders, but if any have inadvertently been overlooked, the Publishers will be pleased to make the necessary arrangements at the first opportunity.

Although every effort has been made to ensure that website addresses are correct at time of going to press, Hodder Education cannot be held responsible for the content of any website mentioned in this book. It is sometimes possible to find a relocated web page by typing in the address of the home page for a website in the URL window of your browser.

Hachette Livre UK's policy is to use papers that are natural, renewable and recyclable products and made from wood grown in sustainable forests. The logging and manufacturing processes are expected to conform to the environmental regulations of the country of origin.

Orders: please contact Bookpoint Ltd, 130 Milton Park, Abingdon, Oxon OX14 4SB. Telephone: (44) 01235 827720. Fax: (44) 01235 400454. Lines are open 9.00–5.00, Monday to Saturday, with a 24-hour message answering service. Visit our website at www.hoddereducation.co.uk

© Gavin Craigen and Joy White 2009
First published in 2001 by
Hodder Education,
An Hachette UK company
338 Euston Road
London NW1 3BH

This second edition first published 2009

Impression number   6
Year   2014

Cover photo: Magnus Fond/Johner Images/Getty Images
Illustrations by Peter Bull/Peter Bull Art Studio
Typeset by Fakenham Prepress Solutions, Fakenham, Norfolk NR21 8NN
Printed in Dubai
A catalogue record for this title is available from the British Library.

ISBN: 978 0340 975 589

Contents

1 Religion and Conflict

2 Religion and Medicine

Contents

3 Religious Expression

4 Authority – Religion and State

1 Religion and Conflict

The Big Picture

Questions to ask

How can communities work together?

How can peace be made and kept and good relations developed?

How can conflict/war be avoided and non-violent protest used?

How can different religions support peace and communities work together?

How important is forgiveness and forgiving?

Is it ever right to fight?

How do people learn to forgive?

Why do the innocent suffer and how can they be helped?

Can a war ever be 'just'?

Key concepts to think about

CONFLICT

INTERFAITH DIALOGUE

JUST WAR | JUST WAR

NON-VIOLENT PROTEST

PACIFISM

BANNED!

RECONCILIATION

Check it out

The definitions used in the Check it out boxes in this chapter are basic outlines only; always add an appropriate example in your explanation, and remember the context is religious believers.

Religious teachings to explore

● Peace
● Suffering
  – The nature of suffering
  – Purpose of suffering
  – Support for those suffering
● Forgiveness and Reconciliation
  – An individual or community working for peace
● Attitudes to conflict and war
  – Just War and equivalents in other religions
● Attitudes to non-violent protest

Peace

Peace is not merely a distant goal that we seek, but a means by which we arrive at that goal. (*Martin Luther King Jr., USA*)

Without justice, peace is nothing but a nice sounding word. (*Dom Helder Camara, Brazil*)

There is no way to peace, peace is the way. (*Mahatma Gandhi, India*)

If you want to make peace with your enemy, you have to work with your enemy. Then he becomes your partner. (*Nelson Mandela, South Africa*)

Peace comes from within. Do not seek it without. (*Siddhartha Gautama, The Buddha*)

Peace is not just the absence of war ... Like a cathedral, peace must be constructed patiently and with unshakable faith. (*Pope John Paul II*)

Peace is a journey of a thousand miles and it must be taken one step at a time. (*Lyndon B. Johnson, former US President*)

Peace is not the product of terror or fear.
Peace is not the silence of cemeteries.
Peace is not the silent result of violent oppression.
Peace is the generous, tranquil contribution of
    all to the good of all.
Peace is dynamism. Peace is generosity,
It is right and duty.
(*Oscar Romero, priest, South America*)

Task

- Design your own logo or image for what you think peace is.

Religious teachings about peace

✝ Christianity

- Retaliation when wronged is not helpful; praying for those who are against you is better.
- Showing love, compassion and kindness towards others is following the example of Jesus.
- Jesus called on people to be 'peacemakers'. (Matthew 5:9)

☾ Islam

- The name 'Islam' comes from a root word meaning peace; and submission to the will of Allah is how peace is produced and maintained.
- It was Allah's command that people live in peace, justice, and responsible brotherhood.
- The Qur'an teaches that Muslims should seek reconciliation and not revenge. (Surah 3:134)

☸ Buddhism

- The first of the five precepts require Buddhists to 'not harm any living thing'.
- Compassion, kindness and love for all living things is at the heart of Buddhism.
- Inner peace, which comes through conquering oneself, is the greatest victory and achievement.

🕎 Judaism

- A Jewish greeting is the word 'Shalom', which means peace, and there is a basic hope of peace becoming a world order in the future. (Isaiah 2:4; Micah 4:3–4)
- In the Talmud it states that three things keep the world safe: peace, truth and judgement.
- Peace is the ideal state, and something to be worked and hoped for; it is the best way for well-being and growth in society.

🕉 Hinduism

- Peace and non-violence are the very basis of *ahimsa*, which should be the main guideline for life.
- Concerning oneself with the inner spiritual life of the atman is the main focus of life; and doing one's duty or *dharma* is of equal importance.
- Maintaining a peaceful society – where the innocent are protected – is important work for Hindus.

☬ Sikhism

- Peace is a gift from God's mercy and so something to be aimed for in life.
- Showing compassion and kindness, and treating others as equals, is a basic principle of Sikh life – and therefore peacefulness is a part of it.
- Sikh adults are required to carry a *kirpan* (sword), even if only symbolically. However, it is only ever to be used in defence.

How can peace be made and kept?

In any friendship or relationship between people, whether just two people, a wider group of friends, or a community, there are many different interests and preferences to be considered. It is very easy for someone or a group to feel left out, or feel that their wishes and ideas are not considered. This means that keeping relationships good and strong needs working at; it needs giving and taking by all the people involved. Peace has to be kept and maintained – it requires effort.

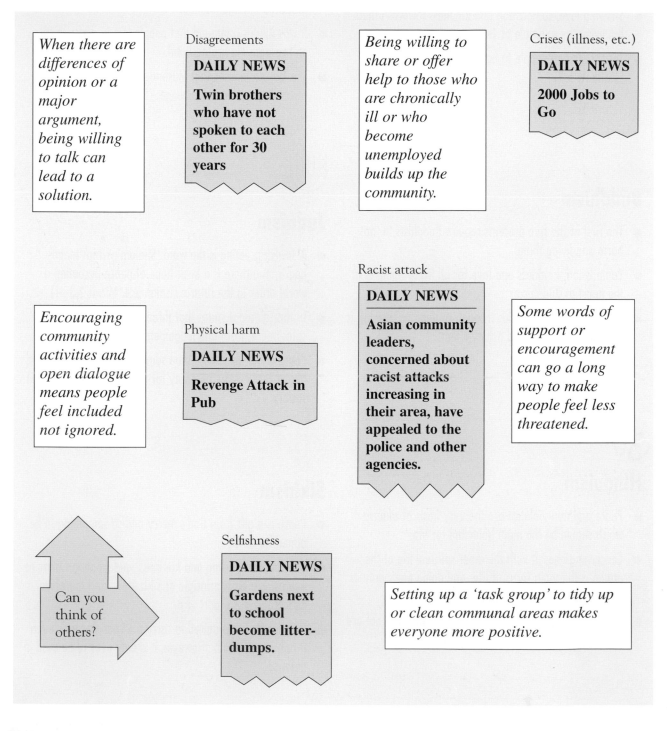

When there are differences of opinion or a major argument, being willing to talk can lead to a solution.

Disagreements

DAILY NEWS

Twin brothers who have not spoken to each other for 30 years

Being willing to share or offer help to those who are chronically ill or who become unemployed builds up the community.

Crises (illness, etc.)

DAILY NEWS

2000 Jobs to Go

Encouraging community activities and open dialogue means people feel included not ignored.

Physical harm

DAILY NEWS

Revenge Attack in Pub

Racist attack

DAILY NEWS

Asian community leaders, concerned about racist attacks increasing in their area, have appealed to the police and other agencies.

Some words of support or encouragement can go a long way to make people feel less threatened.

Can you think of others?

Selfishness

DAILY NEWS

Gardens next to school become litter-dumps.

Setting up a 'task group' to tidy up or clean communal areas makes everyone more positive.

How can good relationships be developed?

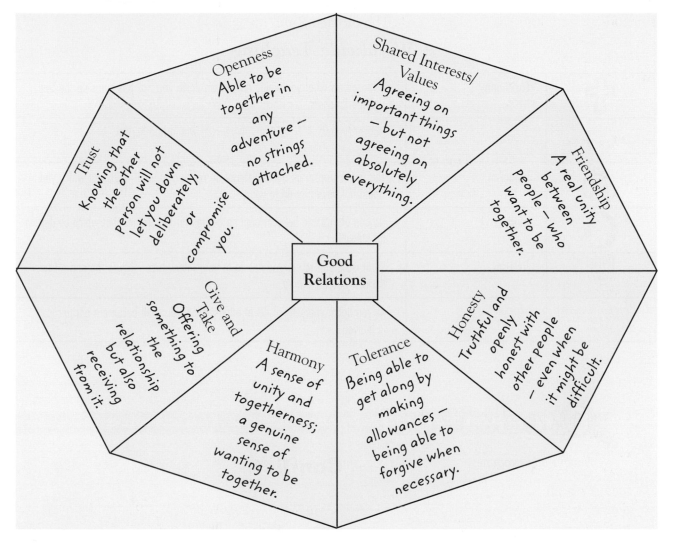

Openness
Able to be together in any adventure – no strings attached.

Shared Interests/Values
Agreeing on important things – but not agreeing on absolutely everything.

Trust
Knowing that the other person will not let you down deliberately; or compromise you.

Friendship
A real unity between people – who want to be together.

Good Relations

Give and Take
Offering something to the relationship but also receiving from it.

Harmony
A sense of unity and togetherness; a genuine sense of wanting to be together.

Tolerance
Being able to get along by making allowances – being able to forgive when necessary.

Honesty
Truthful and openly honest with other people – even when it might be difficult.

People have found that where these feelings (or at least some of them) are common, then relationships and friendships tend to be strong and longer lasting. Without them, the friendship and togetherness can become strained, and may eventually break down.

Task

- Select two of the attitudes from the diagram above and describe a situation for each which reflects that attitude.

- Think about the opposites of the above attitudes – why do you think they lead to difficulties in a relationship?

As the Golden Rule shows below, many religions have the same basic teachings about attitudes to others and to conflict.

The Golden Rule		
		A Worldwide Teaching
✝	**Christianity**	Do to others what you would have them do to you, for this sums up the Law and the Prophets.
☸	Buddhism	Hurt not others in ways that you yourself would find hurtful.
ॐ	Hinduism	This is the sum of all righteousness: do nothing to your neighbour which you would not have him do to you.
☪	Islam	No one of you is a believer until he desires for his brother that which he desires for himself.
🕎	**Judaism**	What is hateful to you, do not do to your fellow men. That is the entire Law; the rest is commentary.
☬	Sikhism	As you deem yourself, so deem others. Then you shall become a partner in heaven.

Check it out

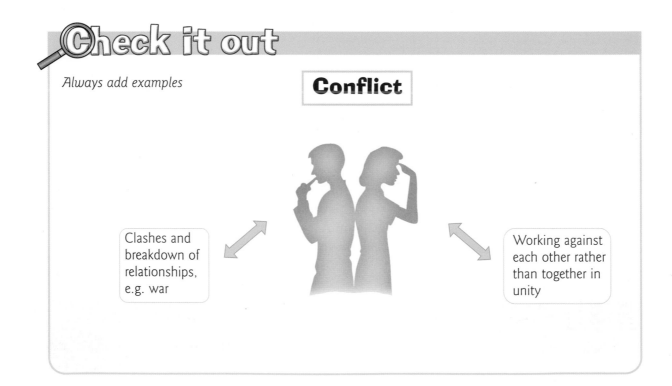

Always add examples

Conflict

Clashes and breakdown of relationships, e.g. war

Working against each other rather than together in unity

Exam Tip

When you are asked to explain the teachings of **two** religious traditions, make sure that you state these clearly, showing where the two traditions you are writing about are different. If your two traditions have very similar teachings on an issue – write that unmistakably. Many candidates do not gain full marks because they fail to make clear what they mean.

Q *Explain from **two** different religious traditions the teaching about attitudes to peace.* [6]

Look at the two answers below, and decide what marks you would give to Answer A and Answer B, and why.

Answer A	Answer B
Roman Catholic teaching about peace is that it comes from Jesus Christ. People should follow his example. Anglicans are the same.	Anglican and Roman Catholic teaching about peace is much the same. They believe that Jesus taught that it was wrong to retaliate when someone mistreated you or said something untrue about you. They also believe that it is important to show love and compassion towards others, even those who might be thought to be our 'enemies'. Both denominations would also point out that Jesus said people should try to be peacemakers.

Conflict and war

Is it ever right to fight?

It isn't right to fight

You said, 'It isn't right to fight,'
But when we watched the news tonight
You shook your fist and said
You wished the tyrant and his cronies dead.
When I asked why,
If it's not right to fight,
You gave a sigh.
You shook your head
And sadly said,
'Sometimes a cause is just,
And, if there is no other way,
Perhaps, you must.'

John Foster, *Standing on the Sidelines*

In responding to the statement, 'It is never right to fight', many religious believers would say there are two sides to the issue:

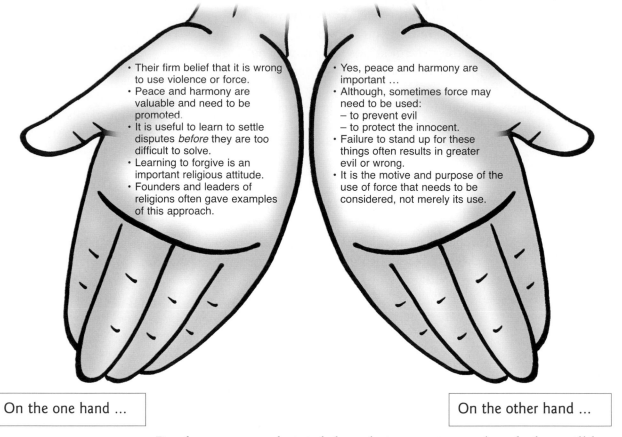

- Their firm belief that it is wrong to use violence or force.
- Peace and harmony are valuable and need to be promoted.
- It is useful to learn to settle disputes *before* they are too difficult to solve.
- Learning to forgive is an important religious attitude.
- Founders and leaders of religions often gave examples of this approach.

- Yes, peace and harmony are important …
- Although, sometimes force may need to be used:
  – to prevent evil
  – to protect the innocent.
- Failure to stand up for these things often results in greater evil or wrong.
- It is the motive and purpose of the use of force that needs to be considered, not merely its use.

On the one hand …

On the other hand …

But for many people it is left to their conscience, though they will be guided by the teachings of their religion, or the values that they have in their life.

Check it out

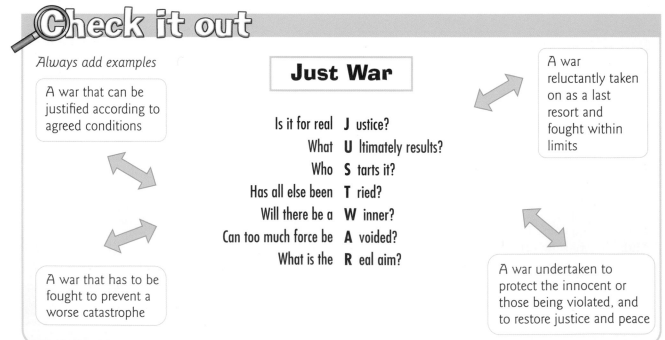

Always add examples

A war that can be justified according to agreed conditions

A war reluctantly taken on as a last resort and fought within limits

Just War

Is it for real **J** ustice?
What **U** ltimately results?
Who **S** tarts it?
Has all else been **T** ried?
Will there be a **W** inner?
Can too much force be **A** voided?
What is the **R** eal aim?

A war that has to be fought to prevent a worse catastrophe

A war undertaken to protect the innocent or those being violated, and to restore justice and peace

What do religions teach about conflict and war?

Some people say that religion is one of the causes of war and violence. They would give examples such as: Roman Catholics and Protestants (Northern Ireland), Christians and Muslims (Lebanon), Buddhists and Hindus (Sri Lanka).

It is not always religion alone in such conflicts – politics, disputes over resources or rights, responding to oppression and prejudice can also be involved.

Many religions teach that violence and war are usually wrong. Some also teach that there are circumstances when believers have to 'take up weapons', because not doing so would result in even worse suffering and injustice.

Each religion has sacred texts and teachings that believers will read and interpret when they are considering issues of conflict. Often within each tradition believers will differ in their opinions.

Christianity ✝

'Do not take revenge on someone who wrongs you ...'
Matthew 5:39

INTERPRETATION:

Although most Christians would want these teachings to be put into practice personally and by society generally, many Christians believe that it is sometimes necessary to go to war. St Augustine put forward the reasons which would justify Christians taking part in a war. These were later developed by St Thomas Aquinas into what has become known as the Just War theory. Many Christians today feel that when these conditions apply a war may be justified:

When there is a just cause.
When declared by a legitimate government.
When the motives are right.
When it is the last resort.
When the innocent are not harmed and the destruction is limited.
When there is a reasonable chance of success.

'As long as the danger of war persists and there is no international authority with the necessary competence and power, governments cannot be denied the right of lawful self-defence, if all peace efforts have failed'.
Catechism of the Catholic Church

For some Christians, defending and protecting others, even at the cost of their own lives, may not only be justified but necessary.

Christianity ✞

'And behold, one of those who were with Jesus stretched out his hand and drew his sword, and struck the slave of the high priest, and cut off his ear. Then Jesus said to him, "Put your sword back into its place; for all who take the sword will perish by the sword."'

Matthew 26:51–52

This means that many Quakers will refuse to join the army but act as Conscientious Objectors and work for disarmament.

Some Quakers are prepared to join medical corps and help those who become wounded.

INTERPRETATION:

Some Christians believe that the words and actions of Jesus show that Christians should not take part in any form of armed conflict. A commonly held belief amongst Quakers (Society of Friends) is that there is 'something of God' in all people and that Quakers should not try to harm them. For many Quakers a declaration made in 1660 has become a central part of their beliefs: 'We utterly deny all outward wars and strife, and fightings with outward weapons, for any end, or under any pretence.'

Sikhism ☬

'Those who beat you with fists, do not give them blows. Go to their homes yourself and kiss their feet.'

Guru Granth Sahib

It must be a last resort with no wish for revenge. The army should be made up of soldiers committed to the cause with a minimum of force being necessary. Any land or property captured during war should be returned afterwards.

INTERPRETATION:

Conflict should always be a last resort. In 1699 Guru Gobind Singh called upon Sikhs to become members of the Khalsa. He fought in defensive battles and said when all other means have failed it is permissible to draw the sword. Dharam Yodh (war in defence of righteousness) sets out the principles for when a Sikh should become involved in a war.

These principles are:

- The war must be the last resort – all other ways to resolve the conflict or issue have been tried, and have failed.
- Revenge or hostility should not play any part.
- The minimum force should be used to bring success.
- Civilians should not be harmed.
- The army must be disciplined, and should not contain mercenaries (i.e. people from other nations paid to be soldiers).
- There should not be looting, confiscating of property or taking over other territories.

Buddhism ✴

'Laying aside the cudgel and the sword he dwells compassionate and kind to all living creatures.'

Digha Nikaya I.4

For this reason many Buddhists will be pacifists and work in non-violent campaigns.

Mahayanna Buddhists, however, would say that if the motive is care for others and is done unselfishly, then it is not a wrong action.

INTERPRETATION:

Central to the Buddha's teachings in the Four Noble Truths and the Eightfold Path are the key beliefs of *ahimsa* (the principle of non-harming) and *metta* (friendliness or loving kindness). For Buddhists all life is interconnected and any action affects one's circumstances in this and future lives (*kamma*). Theravada Buddhists would say that killing is always wrong and brings kammic consequences.

The Dalai Lama, who won the Nobel Peace Prize, refers to the main focus of harmlessness in Buddhism and their commitment to peace when he stated: '*Hatred will not cease by hatred, but by love alone. This is the ancient law.*' The code by which Buddhist monks live allows them to defend themselves if needed, but not to kill – even in self-defence. Even those forms of Buddhism that train followers in martial arts forbids the student from being the aggressor; the whole point of the martial arts learned is to use their techniques to avoid harm, and to use only the amount of force needed to refuse or absorb the violence being shown against them.

Hinduism ॐ

'Heroism, power, determination, resourcefulness, courage in battle, generosity and leadership are the qualities of work for the kshatriyas.'

Krishna's dialogue with Arjuna

Bhagavad Gita 18:43

Armed conflict is allowed if it is to fight against evil and prevents something worse happening.

INTERPRETATION:

Although there is reference to 'battle' in this quote, it is in the context of protecting and defending the innocent. A central belief of Hinduism is *ahimsa* (non-violence) and Hindus are expected to work for peace. It is the *dharma* (main duty) of the kshatriyas to protect the innocent. The word 'kshatriya' means 'who protects from harm'. A true warrior will never hurt the innocent.

So although the use of force is acceptable in self-defence, there are rules in the Rig Veda (6-75:15) about the proper conduct of war:

- arrow tips should not be poisoned
- sick or old people should not be attacked
- women and children should not be attacked
- enemies should not be attacked from behind.

These principles can easily be related to modern-day conflicts, and even Gandhi, who believed that ahimsa was the highest duty of any human being, accepted that there were times when killing another through duty (provided it was done without anger or selfish motives) did not go against ahimsa.

Islam

'And fight in the cause of God those who fight with you, but do not go over the limits; God does not love the aggressors.'

Surah 2:190

INTERPRETATION:

The greater jihad is the personal struggle against all the temptations to do wrong and act against the wishes of Allah. There are clear conditions for military war (the lesser jihad) but the main aim should be to restore peace and freedom.

Islamic guidelines for war that is ethically right, and the conditions for the conduct of such wars, are very clear.

War is permitted:

- in self-defence
- when an Islamic nation is attacked by others
- when another state or nation is oppressing the Muslims in its borders.

Should such a war be entered, then it must be conducted:

- with the minimum force necessary
- in a disciplined manner
- so as to avoid injury to civilians
- without anger
- where prisoners of war are treated humanely.

'Permission to fight is given to those who are attacked, because they have been wronged. Allah has power to help them. They are those who have been unjustly driven from their homes, only because they said: "Our Lord is Allah."'

Surah 22:39–40

Fighting should only be used in defence; it should be the last resort; it should be led by a spiritual leader and civilians, trees, crops and animals should be protected.

Judaism

'You shall not slay them. Would you slay those whom you have taken captive with your sword and with your bow? Set bread and water before them, that they may eat and drink and go to their master.'

2 Kings 6:22

'He shall judge between many peoples, and shall decide for strong nations afar off; and they shall beat their swords into ploughshares, and their spears into pruning hooks; nation shall not lift up sword against nation, neither shall there be war anymore.'

Micah 4:3

Many Jews accept that sometimes wars have to happen but within the Jewish community there are many examples of projects that seek peace and interfaith dialogue.

INTERPRETATION:

Jews regard peace as the ideal state and so the Messianic age is seen in terms of one of peaceful harmony. When warfare happens then it is important to treat those captured justly.

The Jewish tradition is clear that before any war is declared or battle entered into, there must have been attempts to make peace first.

There have been references to three types of war that might be encountered:

- **Obligatory wars** that Jews have been commanded to participate in by God (such as the Biblical examples of fighting against the Canaanites and the Amalekites).
- **Defensive wars** where Jews defend themselves against attacks made on them or their state (and such a war is obligatory too). This would also mean that anticipatory strikes (when a country attacks another because it expects the other to be about to attack) are acceptable – but there needs to be strong evidence to support the action taken.
- **Optional wars** where war or fighting may be undertaken for very good reasons, and where other forms of negotiation or peace making are not possible.

Within many religious traditions there are people who are against all forms of war and use of force or violence. They are often called 'pacifists' – because they believe peace is always the best aim and approach. Such people would refuse to participate in any fighting, even if their government conscripts them into the armed forces. They are called 'conscientious objectors' – because they object to taking part in war on grounds of conscience.

Exam Tip

Using Stimuli to Help Evaluations

On the exam paper there will be a number of pictures that will help you consider the questions. Look at the pictures and consider the evaluation question before you begin the task.

Task

- Having a religious belief cannot help you in times of war. Do you agree? Give reasons to support your answer showing you have thought about more than one point of view. You must refer to religious beliefs in your answer.

- Look back over the religions you have studied. From the information given about religious teachings and interpretations, make a list of arguments for and against the following statement: 'No war can ever be just.' Then prepare a full evaluative answer using the SWAWOS framework on page 15.

Psalm 23 written on a soldier's helmet

Select ...	... specialist language for the issue.	*Choose key terms that you need to use in your answer.*
What do you think and why?	Ask yourself, 'What is the statement saying?' and, 'What do I think about that?' Then write down your own thinking about the issue.	*Read it carefully, think about it sensibly, and write your own thinking clearly.*
Apply religious teaching or example.	Show how religious teaching affects the way you think, or give an example of something from religion that affects the answer you have offered.	*Make sure the links between religious beliefs, teachings and practice are clear.*
What's another point of view?	Think about other views – not necessarily just the opposite view! Comment on them sensitively, and acknowledge their contribution to the debate about the issue; show you understand the other view.	*Make sure you consider other views or ideas clearly and sensitively.*
Offer religious/moral teachings for the other point of view.	Make it clear how religious/moral teachings also affect the alternative view you have referred to. Show that alternative views are also based on what those people believe/value.	*Show clearly that religious beliefs, teachings and practice affect the views people have on the issue.*
Suggest how your response might impact ...	... on the individual and society when making your judgement. Top marks are only awarded to answers that make this impact clear.	*End with a clear conclusion about the impact of your answer or view on individuals and society.*

Exam Tip

How to do Evaluative Questions

Try to follow the simple framework opposite when answering this type of question. This will ensure you meet the criteria in the Levels of Response Grid for AO2 questions, as shown on page 138.

Can a war ever be 'just'?

In answering this question there are differing arguments:

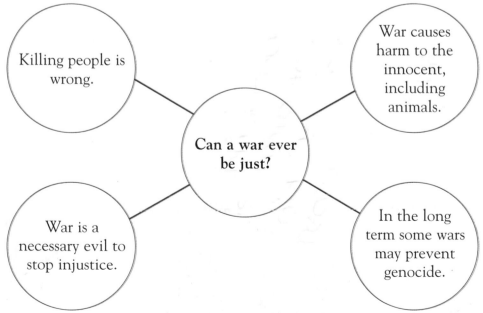

Within a religious tradition believers may have individual views on this issue.

Attitudes to non-violent protest

Non-violent protest is taking some action to stand up against and resist oppression, injustice or to bring about change.

Often the non-violent protestor is more willing to take on suffering themselves in order to make their stand clear and to bring about the change they feel is needed.

Non-violent protest can take many different forms:

Striking

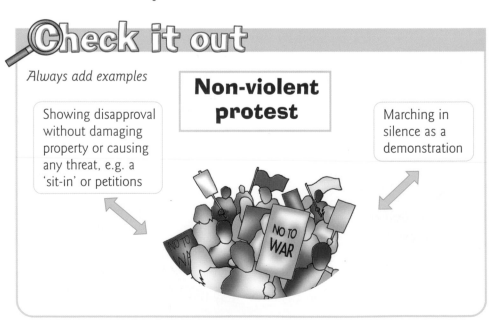

Check it out

Always add examples

Non-violent protest

Showing disapproval without damaging property or causing any threat, e.g. a 'sit-in' or petitions

Marching in silence as a demonstration

Civil disobedience

Other forms of non-violent protest	
Peaceful demonstrations	Picketing
Fasting and hunger strikes	Sit-ins
Blockades	Petitions

Vigils

Exam Tip

Use stimulus provided in the examination paper to help you. Never just describe the pictures or copy headings or words from the stimulus page. The stimulus is there to help you remember the things you have discussed and studied. It should give you ideas to write about and either explain from a religious believer's point of view, or for you to add your own personal ideas.

Task

- Using the stimulus provided for the different forms of non-violent actions (above and page 16), answer the two questions (below) and put into practice the advice in the exam tip.

Q 1. *Explain how religious believers might use non-violent protest.* [4]
2. *'To get things done or changed means you have to fight.' Give two reasons why a religious believer might agree or disagree.* [4]

Religious attitudes to non-violence

Christianity ✟

- Christians generally favour non-violent responses because of Jesus' teaching and example.
- St Paul in Romans 13 talks about Christians obeying governing authorities.
- Non-violence is humane and creative.
- Standing up for justice and equality is expected – despite rejections and abuse received as a result.

Buddhism ✵

- Peace, compassion and calmness are the main aspects of Buddhist living and attitudes.
- Non-harming is also the first of the five precepts – so non-violence is an integral part of not harming others.
- Some Buddhists accept that being willing to commit harmful acts against oneself in order to save or protect others is acceptable.

Hinduism ॐ

- Ahimsa – not harming other living beings – is at the heart of Hinduism; so non-violence is the way preferred.
- Gandhi's example of non-violent direct action inspired many, and achieved much.
- It is important also to work for and maintain peace and justice – and to protect the innocent; this may require force.

Islam ☾

- It is the command of Allah that all live in peace, justice and responsible brotherhood – therefore non-violence is best.
- Reconciliation and forgiveness are taught clearly in the Qur'an.
- However, it may be necessary at times for the striving for justice (*jihad*) to use force and fighting.

Judaism ♉

- Peace and harmony between people – when non-violence is the basis – is hoped for.
- Offers for peace and reconciliation should be made before any use of force or war.
- However, it is right to defend justice and life – even if force and violence are needed.

Sikhism ☬

- Non-violence and peaceful means are the basis of much Sikh action; some Sikhs also believe in *ahimsa* (not harming other living beings).
- Defending the faith, and standing up for justice is also expected – even if it means fighting to do so.

Check it out

Always add examples

Pacifism

BANNED!

The belief that any form of violence or war is unacceptable

Being unwilling to use any force or violence, e.g. by not joining an army

Individuals or communities working for peace

There are many ways to work for or try to keep peace. An important step is often to encourage reconciliation to take place. Whenever there has been conflict, violence or war, there is always a need to rebuild relationships afterwards.

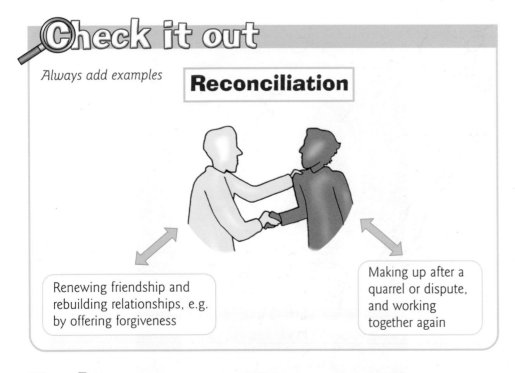

Check it out

Always add examples

Reconciliation

Renewing friendship and rebuilding relationships, e.g. by offering forgiveness

Making up after a quarrel or dispute, and working together again

Task

- Select two of the examples from pages 20–24 and note the motivation, approach and effect of the individuals or communities.

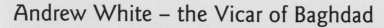

Andrew White – the Vicar of Baghdad

Rev Canon Andrew White is an Anglican priest, who – despite suffering from multiple sclerosis – is Vicar of St George's Church in Baghdad (the only Anglican church still standing in Iraq). He also works as head of the Foundation for Reconciliation in the Middle East, and acts as a link between the United States and leaders in places like Iraq, Israel, Gaza, and the West Bank. He has had success as a hostage negotiator and regularly meets insurgents, terrorists and hostage-takers. His aim is to find common ground among the religious and political groups in these places of conflict, and to bring about reconciliation and peace.

He has been hijacked, kidnapped and held at gunpoint. But he believes that peace can only come when people are willing to talk – especially to those with whom they would rather not talk. His motto is: 'I don't just work with nice people. I work with everyone and treat them as human beings, even the bad guys.'

Look it up

www.frrme.org

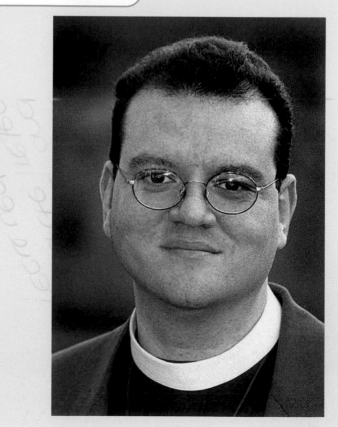

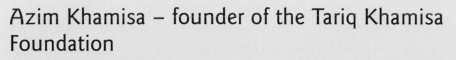

Azim Khamisa – founder of the Tariq Khamisa Foundation

Azim's son Tariq was killed in 1995 while studying in San Diego State University in California. He had been delivering pizzas – a part-time job he had to support his studying. His killer was fourteen-year-old Tony Hicks, a member of a local gang.

After the death of his son, Azim went into the mountains of Southern California, to try to reflect and calm himself. He said: 'There was no solace to be found and I turned to my faith as a Sufi Muslim. For the next few days I survived through prayer and was quickly given the blessing of forgiveness.' So he began to think about tackling the reasons behind his son's death, rather than the boy who had killed his son.

Azim asked to meet the guardian of Tony Hicks, to discuss both their losses. It was from this thinking that the Tariq Khamisa Foundation (TKF) began to emerge.

They decided to work together to establish TKF which has visited over 8 million students to develop a culture of peacemakers and say no to gangs, guns and violence.

 Look it up
www.tkf.org

Tariq Khamisa

Corrymeela

The word 'Corrymeela' means 'Hill of Harmony' and is the name of a charity established over 40 years ago to promote reconciliation and peace-building between Protestants and Roman Catholics in Northern Ireland, by arranging opportunities for meetings and dialogue. Through these experiences of talking and working together it is hoped that the prejudices and fears the two groups have of each other will be changed.

Many of the projects they run involve working with children. One example is from Belfast, where large brick walls had been built to separate the Roman Catholic and Protestant neighbours. At the time the project began, children would often throw bricks over the wall at each other. Through Corrymeela, people from the Protestant and the Roman Catholic groups met to consider what they could do. They ran a children's programme where a clown made the children realise the hurt of being laughed at because of being different. Children from both groups went away together, and through games and workshops, came to be friends. Soon they agreed to stop throwing bricks and stones at each other.

A few days after the project had been completed, the person who had led the programme passed through the same area of Belfast. She saw the children hanging around on the opposite sides of the walls, and asked what they were doing. The children explained that they waited there every day on their way home from school so they could shout hello and greet their friends on the other side.

Look it up
www.corrymeela.org

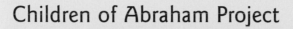

Children of Abraham Project

This project was started by a Jewish woman and a Muslim man who realised that their communities knew little about each other, and that it would aid peace if both sides knew more.

The name *Children of Abraham* reflects that Jews and Muslims share a common spiritual ancestor in Abraham. The project aims to build understanding between Muslims and Jews worldwide through the internet.

Each week, photos of Muslim and Jewish life are explained to help people on both sides understand the different beliefs and practices. Through the chat rooms young people discover they have a lot more in common than they have differences. Frank discussion about difficult subjects such as suicide bombings and military action in the West Bank and Gaza is encourged.

Nadia Sheikh, a member of the Children of Abraham project, said: 'It's something you feel you have to do. You are not only spreading peace and knowledge; you are getting a better understanding. There isn't the possibility you could have a closed mind ever again.'

Look it up

www.childrenofabraham.org

Young people learn about each other's religions

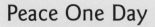

Peace One Day

- Jeremy Gilley is an actor-turned-filmmaker.

- He wanted there to be an annual day of global ceasefire and non-violence with a fixed calendar date and he founded his organisation Peace One Day (POD) to help him do this.

- He filmed his travels and discussions with politicians, United Nations staff and people living in conflict to build a case for an annual Peace Day.

- Finally, in 2001, the United Nations General Assembly decided to designate 21 September as an annual day of global ceasefire and non-violence on the International Day of Peace – Peace Day.

- POD now works to tell the world's people about Peace Day and asks everyone to do something on the Day. Each year Peace Day grows; many millions of people are now involved.

- On Peace Day each year schools, churches and even whole communities arrange displays, services, debates or reflective experiences that try to get people thinking positively about peace, working together to overcome differences and encouraging peace initiatives and attitudes.

- POD gives education packs to schools, and there have been concerts and other large celebrations. In Afghanistan and elsewhere, Jeremy and POD have helped to create the conditions for life-saving activities to take place.

 Look it up

www.peaceoneday.org

Exam Tip

In the exam you will often be expected to explain how a person or communities work together for peace. When answering questions make sure that the details you give are relevant. Use the IMPACT framework below to help you.

Task

- **Select one person who has used or campaigned for non-violence. Complete the following framework to describe the IMPACT of their work and example.**

I dentify ...	the correct name of the person
M ention ...	the religious tradition to which they belong
P récis ...	the context in which they worked
A cknowledge ...	some of the main aspects of their work or example
C onsider ...	how their example demonstrates the teachings of the religious tradition to which they belong
T ell ...	of specific actions or projects that relate to their work and beliefs.

Note

There are lots of other examples of peacemakers – individuals and organisations – on the internet. One interesting example is given below, which has twelve examples of peacemakers from many different traditions who are trying to make a difference.

www.peacemakers.tv/sabet.html

It would also be perfectly possible to use local examples of people or organisations – their involvement in the classroom and discussion with students will help to enhance their ability to describe the work and motivation through the IMPACT formula.

How can different religions support peace by talking to each other?

If communities are going to work together and live in harmony, there needs to be clear understanding of the different groups that live within it, and there needs to be talking and communication between the groups so that they understand each other and know what they all think and aspire towards.

This talking together and sharing of ideas and experiences has been called Interfaith dialogue.

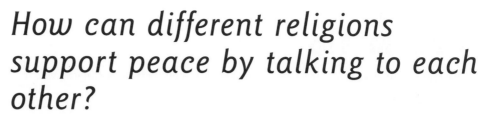

Jews and Muslims creating art for peace

Interfaith dialogue does not mean that the groups all come to share the same views and change their worship or beliefs; they retain their individual thinking and doctrines, but they have learned about each other, in order to respect and understand – not so as to become united together in a new form of religion or belief.

Check it out

Always add examples

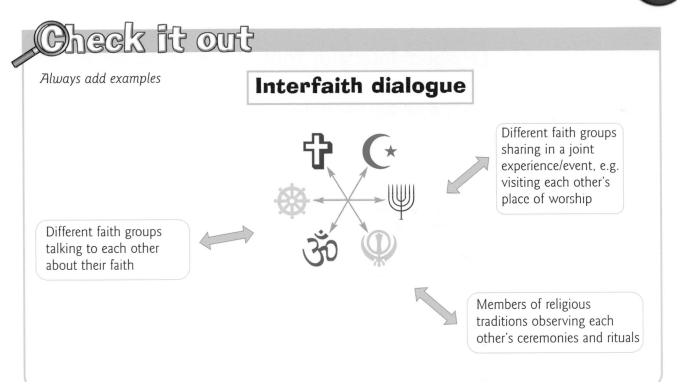

Interfaith dialogue

Different faith groups sharing in a joint experience/event, e.g. visiting each other's place of worship

Different faith groups talking to each other about their faith

Members of religious traditions observing each other's ceremonies and rituals

Neve Shalom/Wahat al-Salam

Neve Shalom/Wahat al-Salam (an oasis of peace) is an area in Israel where Jewish and Arab families live together in peaceful co-existence. It holds many activities where Jewish and Arab children play and learn together.

Look it up

http://nswas.com

Liverpool Interfaith Youth Council Project

The Liverpool Interfaith Youth Council brings together 14–19-year-olds from different faith backgrounds.

The aims of the Youth Council are as follows:

- To promote understanding, respect and positive co-operation.
- To encourage the teenagers to work together to make decisions about their community.
- To develop active citizenship within the local community.
- To develop self-confidence and increase understanding of those with beliefs different from their own.

In order to achieve these aims the Youth Council:

- Hold workshops in which they learn about aspects of each other's faiths.
- Get involved in community projects and get to know people in the community.
- Go on residential trips, visiting places of cultural and historical significance.

Look it up

www.community-spirit.org.uk

How important is forgiveness?

In working for peace and harmony, or when trying to rebuild relationships after differences of opinion, conflict, or hostility, there is a need for forgiveness. Each religion has clear teachings about the importance of forgiveness.

- The teachings of the Buddha concerning Metta
- The second and third of the six perfections
- The actions of the Buddha, for example when he met Angulimala

- Examples of Hindus, for example Gandhi's practice and sayings
- Dharma

- The Teachings of Jesus, for example The Beatitudes; his words from the cross
- The actions of Jesus, for example Zacchaeus
- Examples of Christians forgiving, for example Martin Luther King
- The Lord's Prayer

FORGIVE ONE ANOTHER

- Example of Guru Nanak
- Consistent with the emphasis of overcoming one's ego and being like God
- Adi Granth 1378 – If someone hits you, do not hit him back. Go home – after kissing his feet

- Teachings from the Tenakh, for example treatment of enemies
- Importance of repentance (teshuvah)
- Role of Rosh Hashanah and the ten days of returning
- Only the victim can forgive

- The example of Muhammad
- Rules of War
- Teachings from the Qur'an, for example those who forgive others will be rewarded by Allah (Surah 42:40)
- The belief that Allah will always forgive someone who is truly penitent

Is forgiveness possible?

Are there some situations where it is impossible to forgive? Religions do not suggest that it is easy to forgive – but only that it is far better to do so. Through religious teachings about forgiveness, believers are gaining deeper spiritual awareness.

How do people learn to forgive?

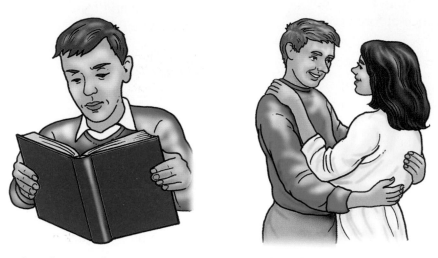

Reading religious teachings   By being forgiven

Many will also hear stories about people – from a variety of religious traditions, and from none – who have shown a remarkable forgiveness in the face of injustice, hatred, or some other harsh experience. All these things help people to not only learn about forgiveness and its importance, but to understand its benefits and value.

Task

- **Think about a time when you had to forgive someone for something. Explain the steps you took to show that forgiveness, and why you thought it important to forgive.**

'I forgive them. I cannot hate. I have to forgive them. Hate is what killed Anthony.'

Gee Walker, mother of murdered Liverpool teenager

Anthony Walker, eighteen, was a member of Grace Family Church in Liverpool, and a youth leader. He was murdered walking his girlfriend to a bus stop. He was attacked by two youths because he was black and later died.

Gee Walker, Anthony's mother, explained that as a Christian it was important to forgive, because of her beliefs in Jesus who showed and taught forgiveness, but also because to not forgive would be insulting to her son Anthony who shared her Christian faith. It was also important to answer racism and hatred with tolerance and love – the only way to conquer and overcome it.

Mrs Walker, in answer to a question about whether she was forgiving her son's murderers for their sake, stated that she was doing it for herself and for her son Anthony. She said:

'Unforgiveness is a heavy weight. It's a big load to carry. I've seen what it does to people. They become bitter, angry. I don't want to be like that. I don't want to be a victim twice over. In my heart I've got love and the pain I feel for Anthony and there's no space for anything else.'

Out of the ashes comes light

The Gobind Sadan Gurdwara in Palermo, New York State, USA was burned to the ground. It had been set alight by local teenagers who thought that the Sikhs who worshipped at the Gurdwara were supporters of the 11 September terrorist attack on the Twin Towers of the World Trade Center in New York.

The whole temple was completely destroyed, but the holy book, the Guru Granth Sahib, survived undamaged. Many of the worshippers at the Gurdwara considered this a miracle, and felt it was a symbol that 'the Light of God's love enshrined in scripture does indeed overcome the darkness of hatred'.

The members of the Gurdwara and Sikh community immediately made a public statement of forgiveness. One of the teenagers involved in the attack, Cassie Hudson, realising the awful things that she had done, was truly sorry and accepted the forgiveness offered by the Sikh community. Together they began the rebuilding process.

Finally, after the slow process of showing love, forgiveness and respect, a new temple was built and re-dedicated. The Director of Public Relations at the Gurdwara, Ralph Singh, said: 'this building rose out of the ashes of hatred and, in its opening, is symbolic of love'.

The Guru Granth Sahib survived the fire undamaged

The nature of suffering

When people suffer they often wonder, 'why?'

> Why me, and not someone else?

> Why has this happened at all?

> What have we done to deserve this?

For as many different types of suffering there are as many different reasons.

Why people suffer is a question known as an 'ultimate question'. That means a question that asks about things that are really concerning fundamental principles in life itself.

When people consider the causes of suffering, there are many different beliefs. For some people, suffering is connected with good and evil, and the balance between these in their own lives, and in the world as a whole. This means that they see some of the suffering as being from their own decisions and actions, but also that some of it is beyond themselves and their own actions and thinking. Every day newspapers and television show us how many people suffer through no fault of their own. Many believers consider that innocent suffering can have a divine purpose and that it is impossible for all life to have no experiences of suffering.

So in the world in which we live, some people will experience suffering that does not seem deserved – it is the result of outcomes and actions for which they are not directly responsible.

33

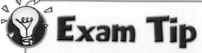

Exam Tip

When a question asks about how something might help religious believers, it is important to remember two things:

- Make sure your answer is *in the context of religious believers*. Don't just write about anyone or anything connected with the idea.
- Select key ideas and, if possible, key words in religion that might be relevant to the particular topic or issue.

Religious teachings on suffering

Christianity ✝ on suffering

For Christians, suffering is seen to have entered the world through the God-given ability of free will. Many would see the story of the creation in Genesis as stating clearly that humans were created with the ability to know and worship God, and to look after the world as his stewards. However, there was a free choice to accept or reject following God's ways. The story of 'the fall' is seen to illustrate the choice to be selfish or self-centred (and so do wrong or sin), rather than to choose the path of willing obedience (and so do right, or good). The idea that humanity finds it easier to choose the selfish way is caused by what is known as 'original sin'. Christians believe that this indicates that human nature is not perfect, but that through faith and discipline, it can overcome the tendency to sin.

As a result, this free will can also lead to suffering, in the sense that there is 'moral' evil in the world – where people choose to do things that will lead to pain or suffering, for themselves or others. Evangelical Christians, and those in denominations such as Pentecostal and Apostolic, would say in addition, that as a result of human sin, the perfect world God created has become contaminated, and so there will also be 'natural' evil – where the natural events of the earth and its elements sometimes lead to suffering or disaster. Others might say that it is also finite – that is, having limits; so there are bound to be accidents, death and decay.

But most Christians also believe that God is neither ignorant nor unfeeling about the suffering of humanity. Indeed, they would say that he is compassionate and understanding, and does bring good out of suffering. Christians see that, with faith and trust in God, suffering can help to develop people's character, their inner strength and their ability to overcome suffering, and succeed in the face of it.

The story of Job is a classic example to which Christians refer. You can read about this in the section on Judaism (see page 37).

Christianity ☩ on suffering

Many Christians would also refer to the example of Jesus, who being God in the flesh, still chose to endure suffering and pain, in order to achieve a greater good.

Christian teaching is that Jesus was the perfect man because he was also God, and as such did not deserve to be put to death on the cross. However, his death and resurrection were to bring an end to death and suffering forever, because Jesus took the punishment for sin, and opened a way to God and his forgiveness. His resurrection offers a certain hope, and the promise of a new heaven and earth.

In the same way, Christians would also see that suffering is a way of participating in the saving work of Jesus, and the Roman Catholic catechism states this point.

Christ of St John of the Cross painted in 1951 by Salvador Dali

Buddhism ☸ on suffering

The truth of suffering is the basic truth of Buddhism. It was an essential part of Siddhartha's enlightenment that he recognised the role of Maya-illusion. The Four Noble Truths show that:

- All is *dukkha* (suffering)
- The cause of suffering is craving/greed and desire
- This can be stopped
- The way to stop it is to follow the Eightfold Path.

Many of the Buddha's actions were to help others understand about dukkha. An example of this can be found in the story of Kisagotami. When Kisa finds her baby has died she goes to the Buddha to find help.

K: Please help me and bring my baby back to life.

B: Fetch a mustard seed from a house where no one has suffered.

K: Now I understand; everyone faces suffering in their life.

35

Hinduism ॐ on suffering

Hindus consider goodness and evil as parts of life coming from God. This is why the god Kali is believed to be good as well as evil as by causing suffering she encourages people to be detached as she constantly destroys the earthly pleasures that people enjoy so much.

Sometimes suffering is considered as part of one of the god's actions and so Hindus try to keep the deities happy. Shiva is considered the lord of destruction and carries a thunderbolt while driving his chariot. He is often portrayed as Nataraja stamping out the devil and wearing a serpent around his neck, and a garland of skulls. Hindus often blame Shiva for natural disasters such as earthquakes, floods and hurricanes.

Hindus believe that to escape suffering, it is important not to become attached to worldly goods which can be an illusion or maya. The Puranas suggest that suffering is a result of people's sinful actions (*papa*) in previous reincarnations – this is the law of karma.

Most Hindus want to achieve *Moksha*, which is the final release or liberation that will free them from any further suffering.

Shiva

Islam ☾ on suffering

For Muslims, everything that happens is part of the will and plan (*qadr*) of Allah. This means that suffering and hardship are part of Allah's great plan, even though people may not be able to see or understand that. The fact is, in Islam, Allah's knowledge is greater than humans, and humans will never be able to comprehend Allah's will and purpose.

Basic to Islamic teaching is the idea that life itself is a test. Humans are given life, the created world and other people for which to care. The purpose of Islam is to enable people to achieve this responsibility. In this way, suffering itself is a kind of test; a proving of one's faith; a showing of one's resistance to the tempting of Satan (*Shaytan*; or *Iblis*).

Good can, however result from suffering, because it is a greater good when people resist temptation, and follow in the way of the Prophet Muhammad. Muslims believe he is the model example for humans to follow.

Shaytan being defeated

But Allah is also known as *Ar-Rahman* (The Merciful), *Ar-Rahim* (The Compassionate), and *Al-Karim* (The Generous), and so those who resist Shaytan, and follow the way laid down, will be rewarded in the afterlife.

Judaism ♆ on suffering

In one sense, suffering results from the presence of free will. The description in Genesis explains that God gave humanity free will, and in so doing, gave them the potential for choosing to do either good or evil. In another sense, suffering comes from God too, as he can use it as a way of discipline, as a form of punishment for wrongdoing, as a kind of test, or a way of returning to God.

Satan Smiting Job by William Blake

The story of Job shows that someone who is a holy and good-living person can go from great success to loss and tragedy for no reason. Job's friends consider that his suffering was a result of past sins. When Job questions God, he does not give direct answers, but challenges him as to how he can question what he does. Job has to accept that God has control, even though he may not, at that time, be able to understand why this suffering is happening to him. Jews consider God to be just, merciful and holy – so it is wrong to question him.

As the story of Job states (28:28):

> The fear of the Lord that is wisdom; And to depart from evil is understanding.'

Throughout history many Jews have been persecuted for their beliefs.

Although Jewish scriptures often portray Satan as an adversary, in the Apocrypha, Satan is portrayed as representing the forces of evil. Yetzar Ha Ra is the selfish desire to do bad things, but is not considered evil in itself.

Most Jews believe that death is not the end, but the soul continues. It is believed that God is the judge, and evil will be punished. During the ten days leading up to Yom Kippur, Jews have the chance to reflect on their misdeeds and to seek atonement.

Throughout history Jews have waited and hoped for the coming of the Mashiach (Messiah) but the Messianic Age has not yet dawned.

Sikhism  on suffering

Many Sikhs consider suffering as the result of human actions (*haumai*), and are not to be blamed on God, even though everything which happens is within his will. Because humans have the ability to know right from wrong, and so choose between them, it is open to them to follow after God's heart and learn to serve others. The Adi Granth recommends that we should give up goods which cannot accompany us after death and concentrate instead on seeking spiritual wealth and inner qualities. In seeking these, the cycle of existence can be broken, and lead to liberation (*mukti*).

There are, however obstacles to achieving *mukti*:

- *Maya*: sometimes called illusion, which results in a focusing on worldly things
- *Manmukh*: or self-centredness, as opposed to God-centredness
- The five evils:
  - *Kam* – lust
  - *Lobh* – covetousness, or greed
  - *Moh* – attachment to worldly things and pleasures
  - *Krodh* – anger
  - *Ahankar* – pride or arrogance

In the Adi Granth, Guru Nanak reflects to himself that it is futile to ask for pleasure when suffering comes, for both are robes that must be worn. But it is possible – and Sikhs should strive for it – to rise above suffering and gain release through obedience and trust in God.

He is the One God, who is eternal truth, creator, who is timeless, immanent, self-existent and beyond the cycle of birth and death.

Sikhs see the soul as a minute spark of the Eternal Soul, and so it will never die. Death is not the end, but the beginning of another phase. So, a combination of good works and religious acts of devotion help one's rebirth.

Task

Look back carefully at the information on the two religious traditions you are studying. For each of the religions make a list of bullet points of the important aspects about the two things below from the information you have read, and the discussions you will have taken part in:

- **The nature of suffering.**
- **The purpose of suffering.**

How
can
those
suffering
be helped?

Support for those suffering

For all religions it is believed that it is important to try to help those suffering around them. Every religious tradition has organisations that support others in a number of practical and spiritual ways.

(You can read about some examples on pages 69–75 in Chapter 3.)

Supporting people who are suffering or in need can take many different forms, and many religious communities and religious organisations offer different examples and combinations of them.

• Look at the range of support activities on this and the next page, and think about why people from the two religious traditions you are studying might want to be involved in these activities, or arrange for them to be funded. Draw up your own table to help you remember. Add more lines if you need them.

Religion:	Activity to support those suffering	Benefits or outcomes	Motivation
Religious tradition 1			
Religious tradition 2			

Holding a special prayer vigil

Training sessions

Medical care and support

Providing clothing

Praying as an individual

Providing hot meals

Praying as a community

Fund-raising events

Counselling

Agriculture development

Education

Rehabilitation programmes

Disaster relief

Sheltered housing

Providing clean, safe water

Building work

Temporary accommodation

As well as the examples given on pages 69–75 in Chapter 3, why not check out others, such as:

Christian: Christian Aid Tearfund Christian Response to Eastern Europe Leprosy Mission Yedall Bridges	**Buddhist:** Rokpa Tzu Chi	**Hindu:** Hindu Aid ISKCON Food for Life
	Islamic: Islamic Aid	**Jewish:** British ORT Chai Cancer Centre Friends of Tikva Odessa
	Sikh: Sikhcess	

Exam Tip

To achieve a high level mark you will be required to use a wide range of religious language terms. When you complete the Test it Out below, use as many words as you can from this table:

conflict	interfaith dialogue	Just War
pacifism	reconciliation	sacred texts
community	The Golden Rule	forgiveness

Also use specific terms from the religious traditions you have studied.

TEST IT OUT

(a) *Explain what religious believers mean by 'non-violent protest'.* [2]

(b) *Explain how having a religious faith might help believers when they are suffering.* [4]

(c) *'All religious believers are committed to peace.' Give* **two** *reasons why a religious believer might agree or disagree with this statement.* [4]

(d) *Explain from* **two** *different religious traditions the teaching about the nature of suffering.* [6]

(e) *'There can never be a just war.' Do you agree? Give reasons or evidence for your answer, showing that you have thought about more than one point of view. You must refer to religious beliefs in your answer.* [8]

2 Religion and Medicine

The Big Picture

Questions to ask

Is it right to spend so much money on IVF when people are starving in the world?

Should people have free will to make life/death decisions?

What are the moral and ethical issues/dilemmas in life and death decisions and because of scientific advancements?

Is it ever right to end someone's life?

Why is life so special?

What are the rights of the unborn child?

How does a religion help or hinder people making decisions?

Whose life is it anyway?

Key concepts to think about ▼

CONSCIENCE	
FREE WILL	
HIPPOCRATIC OATH	
MEDICAL ETHICS	
QUALITY OF LIFE	
SANCTITY OF LIFE	

Check it out

The definitions used in the Check it out boxes in this chapter are basic outlines only; always add an appropriate example in your explanation, and remember the context is religious believers.

Religious teachings to explore

- The sanctity of life
- Medical ethics
  - Support in making decisions about medical ethics
- Abortion
- Euthanasia
- IVF (In-vitro fertilisation)

> 'A man is ethical only when life, as such, is sacred to him, that of plants and animals as that of his fellow men, and when he devotes himself helpfully to all life that is in need of help.'
>
> Albert Schweitzer

Why is life so special?

For many people living things are very special simply because life is a mystery. We know how people and animals are born, and we know what 'ingredients' there are in physical bodies. We know all about the workings of the human and animal bodies, and even a great deal about the workings of our brains and minds, our memories and emotions. But, the one thing that we still do not know is exactly what makes something alive.

No one is able to create life, although by using the 'ingredients' of sperm and ovum it is possible to stimulate fertilised cells. Eventually, though, the growing embryo needs to be implanted into a womb in order for it to grow and develop.

All the world religions teach that life is special and should be protected and valued – for each life is unique and valuable beyond any price or measure.

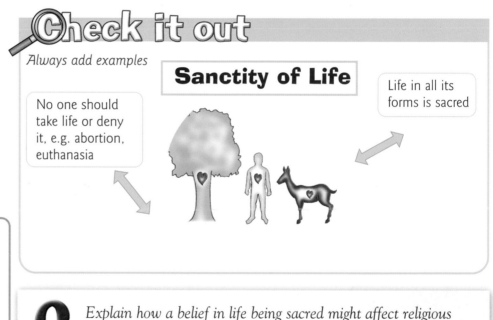

Check it out

Always add examples

Sanctity of Life

No one should take life or deny it, e.g. abortion, euthanasia

Life in all its forms is sacred

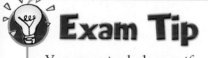

Exam Tip

You must include specific religious content in your answers to questions about the teachings or practices of religious traditions, even though it seems easier to write about more general cultural traditions or understandings.

Q *Explain how a belief in life being sacred might affect religious believers.* [4]

Look at the answer below. Using the Levels of Response Grids (AO1) on page 137, decide what mark to give the answer, and explain why. Then rewrite the answer so that it can gain full marks. Note what you are adding – and learn to always include these elements in your answers to these questions.

> Because many believers see life as sacred they believe it is a gift from God, so it belongs to him. So all life is precious and should not be wasted.

Sanctity of Life

Sanctity of Life in Christianity ✝	Sanctity of Life in Buddhism ☸	Sanctity of Life in Hinduism ॐ
• God is interested and involved in each human's life. • Life is sacred and a gift from God. • Only God should take life away. • Jesus showed in his teaching that all life should be valued.	• From the moment of conception an embryo is a living being. • All forms of life are caught in the cycle of existence (*samsara*), and are affected by actions and their karma (*kamma*). • Being born as a human is a very precious thing, and has the potential for completion and nirvana.	• The soul is present in all species of life. • All life is sacred and worthy of the highest respect. • Everything that lives and grows is interconnected. • Where there is life or soul there is atman. • At death the soul enters another body.

Sanctity of Life in Islam ☪	Sanctity of Life in Judaism 🕎	Sanctity of Life in Sikhism ☬
• Every soul has been created by Allah. • Allah has a plan for each life. • No one has the right to take their own or anyone else's life.	• Life is sacred and a gift from God. • *Pukuach nefesh* shows the importance of putting aside laws to save life.	• Life is sacred, and should never be violated. • Life begins at conception.

Q Explain what religious believers mean by the 'sanctity of life'. [2]

Look at the answers below, and you will see a full answer and a part answer; you should always aim to show your answer is about religious believers and what they think.

Exam Tip

When giving an answer that requires a definition, be precise in what you say. Many candidates do not gain full marks because they repeat words or phrases within their answer, or because they do not cover the essential points of a definition. *You must also write your answer in the context of religious believers, so make sure you make that clear in your answer.*

Answer A	Answer B
Life is sacred and precious. No one should take it away from anyone else.	The belief that all life is sacred, because it is given by God, and therefore is precious. Because it is God-given it is so valuable, that no one should take that life away – only God himself has that right.

The belief in the sanctity of life raises many moral issues:

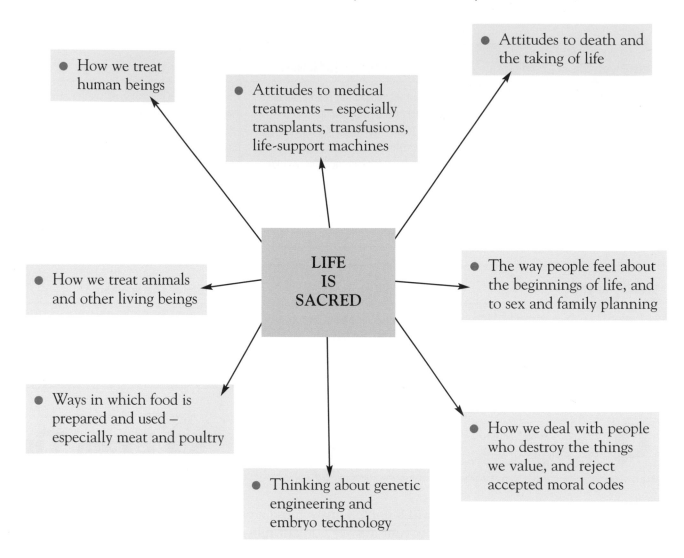

- How we treat human beings

- Attitudes to medical treatments – especially transplants, transfusions, life-support machines

- Attitudes to death and the taking of life

- How we treat animals and other living beings

LIFE IS SACRED

- The way people feel about the beginnings of life, and to sex and family planning

- Ways in which food is prepared and used – especially meat and poultry

- Thinking about genetic engineering and embryo technology

- How we deal with people who destroy the things we value, and reject accepted moral codes

Check it out

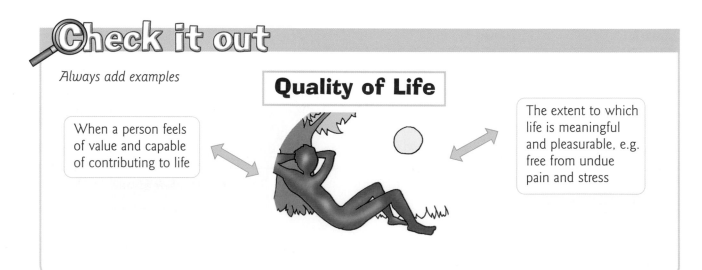

Always add examples

Quality of Life

When a person feels of value and capable of contributing to life

The extent to which life is meaningful and pleasurable, e.g. free from undue pain and stress

Medical and ethical decisions? Scientific advancements?

As a result of advances in scientific knowledge and the development in technology, questions about life and death have become much more complex. In the past, people died of diseases and accidents, and there was little that could be done to help them. Today, treatment of diseases and the amazing work of trauma specialists have made it possible for people to survive against all odds. But such medical achievements raise big ethical questions:

- When to turn off a life-support machine? Who decides?
- Should you always try to preserve life?
- Is it right to respect a patient's wishes or beliefs?
- Should donating organs be made compulsory?

Task

- Answer two of the questions below, giving reasons or evidence for your answers.

Check it out

Always add examples

Medical ethics

A code of conduct in identifying what is good medicine or treatment

The process of deciding what is good and acceptable in medicine, e.g. through conscience

Some questions to be asked:

- Is this playing God?
- What happens to the other embryos?
- When does life begin?

A New Approach to Family Planning

In about fifteen years' time it will not be unusual for a single woman to freeze her eggs. Then, when she has a firm foothold in her career, has met Mr Right and feels ready to start a family, she will have one of her eggs thawed, fertilised with her partner's sperm, and the embryo implanted for pregnancy. A year or so later she can do the same again, or whenever it is convenient for her to have another child. Under the Human Rights Act she will be entitled to do this for free.

- Should there be an age restriction?
- Is it murder if the other embryos are destroyed?
- Is technology being abused?
- What if Mr Right is never found?

Some scientific advancements that raise ethical questions

Testing drugs

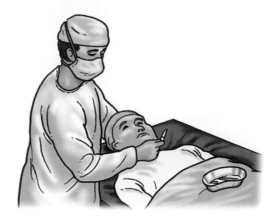

Plastic surgery for cosmetic purposes

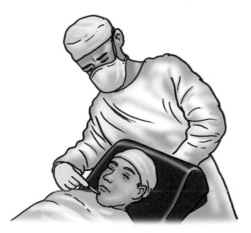

Surgical implants

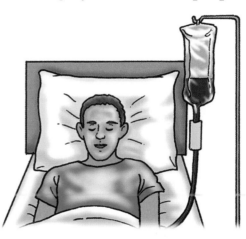

Blood transfusions

> We need a boy who will have the cells that can cure our first son's illness.

Fertility treatment

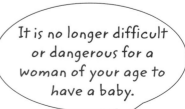

> It is no longer difficult or dangerous for a woman of your age to have a baby.

How does a religion help or hinder people making decisions?

From the work that you have been doing so far, you can see how religious beliefs and teachings affect the things people have to make decisions about. Life/death decisions are obviously never easy to make, but how far does a religion help or hinder a person when making these decisions?

On the one hand, a religious faith, and principles by which to live, could make the decision easier, as there is a framework or criteria by which to decide. To some extent, the agonising is taken away, as the teachings and beliefs give clear guidance and direction.

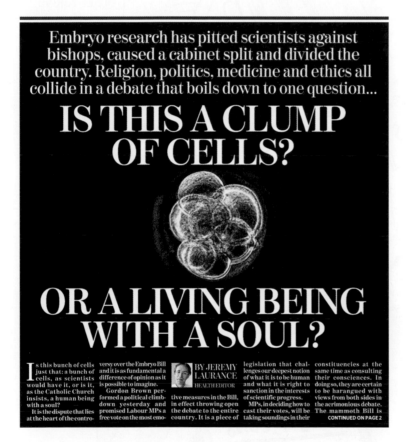

Embryo research has pitted scientists against bishops, caused a cabinet split and divided the country. Religion, politics, medicine and ethics all collide in a debate that boils down to one question...

IS THIS A CLUMP OF CELLS?

OR A LIVING BEING WITH A SOUL?

Is this bunch of cells just that: a bunch of cells, as scientists would have it, or is it, as the Catholic Church insists, a human being with a soul?

It is the dispute that lies at the heart of the contro-versy over the Embryo Bill and it is as fundamental a difference of opinion as it is possible to imagine.

Gordon Brown per-formed a political climb-down yesterday and promised Labour MPs a free vote on the most emo-

BY JEREMY LAURANCE
HEALTH EDITOR

tive measures in the Bill, in effect throwing open the debate to the entire country. It is a piece of legislation that chal-lenges our deepest notion of what it is to be human and what it is right to sanction in the interests of scientific progress.

MPs, in deciding how to cast their votes, will be taking soundings in their constituencies at the same time as consulting their consciences. In doing so, they are certain to be harangued with views from both sides in the acrimonious debate. The mammoth Bill is CONTINUED ON PAGE 2

On the other hand, for a lot of the decisions people have to make today – on issues like abortion, euthanasia, IVF treatments, transplants, and the other modern medical possibilities – there are no clear religious teachings as such. So it is more difficult to make decisions, and to apply other teachings and beliefs to them; that is one of the reasons why there are varying views within religious traditions on these issues.

That is why most religions and their leaders and teachers, advise using a range of methods – as shown in the diagram on the next page – in arriving at a decision.

So how does a believer decide when there is no specific teaching in religious traditions about modern medical issues?

Most religious traditions would probably expect believers to use some of the following methods to arrive at a sensible and acceptable conclusion:

Search the sacred texts for references or beliefs that may relate to the issue.

Think about ultimate principles in the religion that will have an impact on the issue.

Analyse intentions, and measure them against other relevant teachings.

How do believers decide what is right in modern medical ethics?

Discuss the matter with other believers, and with 'experts' in the religion and the issue.

Pray about the issues involved and seek guidance directly from God.

Consider the effects on themselves and others, and on society as a whole, and weigh up whether these are compatible with basic beliefs.

Should people have free will to make life/death decisions?

For many religious believers, decisions about life/death decisions will not only include consideration of religious teachings and beliefs, but will also be affected by their conscience.

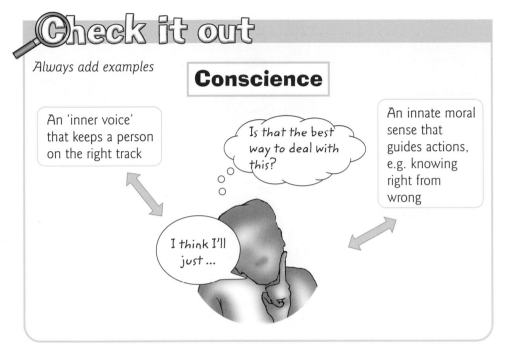

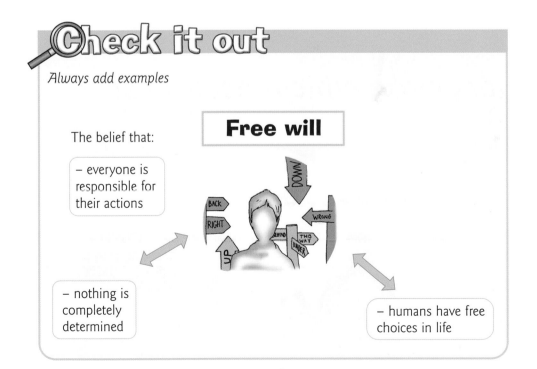

Different people have different views on this subject as shown below.

I don't agree with all this intervention of science — it's like playing God.

Life is not held sacred any more. People forget about the sanctity of life.

When I think of the suffering my aunt went through I realise it doesn't matter how long you live — it's the quality of life that matters.

A baby is a human being from the moment of conception. I don't believe in abortion.

How do doctors make ethical decisions?

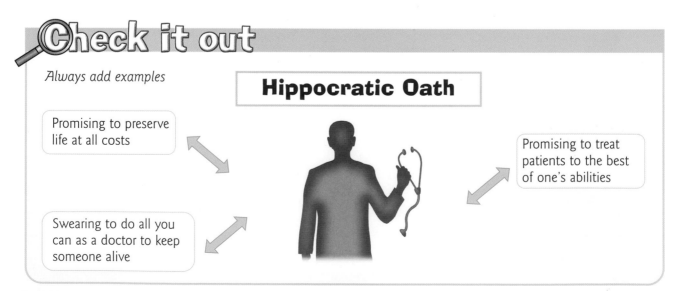

Check it out

Always add examples

Hippocratic Oath

Promising to preserve life at all costs

Promising to treat patients to the best of one's abilities

Swearing to do all you can as a doctor to keep someone alive

Doctors take what is called the 'Hippocratic Oath'. This is a solemn promise to:

- preserve life at all costs
- treat patients to the best of one's abilities
- never cause intentional harm, and
- maintain patient confidentiality.

It has a big impact on the way doctors respond to some of the medical issues and circumstances they face. It is important for them to weigh up the extent to which they are keeping true to the Hippocratic Oath, and also thinking of the patient's best interests, not just in terms of the short-term situation that has brought the patient into their care.

They also have to consider the interests of the family and relatives of the patient, and the impact their treatment, or lack of certain treatments, might have.

In arriving at their decision, they have to consider all the medical evidence, all the ethical issues involved, and all the interests of the patient and their family. Sometimes it is not simply a medical matter – there are wide and far-reaching implications in the options the doctor has to consider and decide on.

Jehovah's Witness died after refusing blood

A woman who refused a blood transfusion died because she chose her faith over her life, an inquest heard. Alison Mallender, a 44-year-old Jehovah's Witness, had been admitted to hospital for a routine operation.

After years of severe abdominal pain, the mother of one was looking forward to surgery and relief from constant discomfort. But the day before the operation, she had made it clear she would not want to accept a blood transfusion. Jehovah's Witnesses see blood as sacred and believe it is God's will that it should not be shared.

During the three-hour operation, surgeons encountered a series of complications. Mrs Mallender's abdominal organs were stuck together following a previous operation and she had started to bleed heavily. For three hours the surgeons battled to separate her organs. But during the process, she suffered a tear to her small bowel and lost a lot of blood.

Later, in intensive care, she was given drugs to try to counteract the blood loss – but on 11 June she lost her fight for life.

Adapted from the *Daily Mail*, 29 December 2006

Stem-cell baby born to cure brother of a killer illness sparks clash with Catholics

Baby Javier was born in Spain through stem-cell selection specifically so that his older brother can be cured. Brother Andrés suffers from congenital anaemia, and the process of screening stem cells in the embryos before birth has led to the chance for material from the umbilical cord of Baby Javier to help cure his brother's anaemia through bone marrow transplants. The stem-cell screening ensured that the baby to be born would have the right stem-cells.

To many Roman Catholics, the process of deliberately screening and selecting fertilised embryos so as to discard those not suitable is unacceptable, even if in the cause of saving another's life. As well as being concerned at what they see as killing one life to save another, they feel that the 'engineered' manner of the birth is degrading to the person, and may well haunt them later in life.

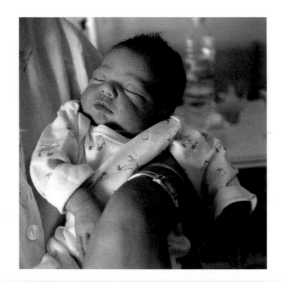

Q *'Decisions in medical ethics must always depend on the situation.' Do you agree? Give reasons or evidence for your answer showing that you have thought about more than one point of view. You must include reference to religious beliefs.* [8]

Use the SWAWOS framework on page 15 to complete a full answer.

Whose choice is it? Abortion

To many people the issue of abortion, although it is often a matter of conscience, is to do with choice and rights:

- The choices and rights of the mother, and whether she wants and is able to have the baby.
- The rights of the child not yet born, to be alive and grow independently.
- The choice about making decisions in accordance with one's own conscience.
- The right of religious believers to consider how their beliefs impact on such an issue.

As with many issues, it is not always simply a matter of making up your own mind – there are other people's views to consider:

> It's my choice. I can't have a baby now – it will ruin my career.

> Hang on a minute – it's partly my child too. I'm sure we can work something out together.

> You need to think of the long-term effects of an abortion, as well as what seems important now.

> I want to stand by my sister; but I really hate the idea of her having an abortion.

> But what about us? We don't believe it is right to take away a life!

> As a neighbour, I think she should just make up her own mind! She's the one who'll have the baby anyway.

> As your religious leader, I urge you to consider the principles of the sanctity of life before reaching a decision.

Deciding what to do as a believer

CHRISTIANITY

- There is no single Christian view on abortion, and individual Christians differ in their response, sometimes even with the 'official stance' of their particular denomination.
- Generally, Christians do have concerns about abortion, because of their beliefs in:
  – The sanctity of life
  – People being in the image of God
  – That all life – whatever form – is precious and purposeful, and so sacred.
- Roman Catholic Churches and Orthodox Churches generally forbid abortion under any circumstances, because they believe that life is sacred and God-given.
- Other Christian Churches tend to be against abortion carried out for social reasons, but accept that in some instances it may be a preferred choice (such as when having to decide between the life of the mother or the child).
- Many Evangelical Protestants are supporters of a Pro-Life stance, and would tend to be against abortion in principle, although acknowledge that there are some specific circumstances that may make it allowable.
- Many Christian denominations leave it open to individual Christians to determine for themselves whether or not abortion is right in their own particular circumstances.

CASE STUDY

Sioned is eighteen, and is working in a company that produces medicines and treatments for chemists and hospitals.

1 She has done well since leaving school.
2 She hopes to continue and get promotion.
3 She has a steady boyfriend, David.
4 They hope one day to marry.
5 David is at university.
6 He is studying religion and hopes to become a teacher.

Sioned has just discovered she is pregnant, and is trying to decide what to do. She and David are both believers. Sioned is thinking of having an abortion, and is wondering whether their religion would let them do so. She writes to a problem page in a magazine to ask for help.

BUDDHISM

- No human should be killed, and this includes the foetus.
- An exception would be when the pregnancy is a source of intense suffering for some members of the family, or when the mother's life is at risk, or the life of the child is going to be seriously handicapped.
- The Five Precepts should be used as guiding principles, and so each individual must make their own decision about their own circumstances.
- Abortion can be seen as breaking the First Precept, as it is cutting off a 'precious human rebirth', which is seen as beginning at conception.
- Bad karma from an abortion is said to vary according to the size of the foetus.
- Some groups, motivated by the principle of compassion, do attach a particular significance to birth.

SIKHISM

- Abortion is morally wrong, because life begins at conception.
- The sanctity of life should never be violated.
- Conception following rape is regarded by some as a possible justification for an abortion.
- A child likely to be born deformed is not usually regarded as sufficient grounds for an abortion, although some Sikhs do recognise the right of parents to decide for themselves in this situation.

Protesters fight to halt 'party of death' aboard abortion ship

Anti-abortion campaigners threatened to gate-crash the Dutch 'abortion ship' *Aurora* and prevent it docking in the Spanish port of Valencia. About 400 protesters gathered. The ship offers free terminations, and takes its passengers out into international waters to perform the abortions – thus providing a means of getting round the strict Spanish laws on abortion.

Feminist groups behind the *Aurora* mission hope to highlight the calls for reform of Spain's strict anti-abortion laws.

Adapted from *The Times*, 17 October 2008

HINDUISM

- All life is sacred and there should be no interference in natural processes.
- The source of all life forms is God, and so should be treated with the highest respect.
- Abortion is against *ahimsa* (harmlessness).
- Some would allow abortion for strict medical reasons (i.e. saving the life of the mother).
- Some believe that the foetus has no shape or personality until the fifth month of pregnancy, so can be aborted before if there are good reasons.
- Others would argue that it is an acceptable method of ending unwanted pregnancy, and therefore is a kind of birth control; recognising the legality of abortions in India, as long as they take place in Government clinics.

JUDAISM

- God is the creator, and he alone can take life.
- Life is God's greatest gift, and it should be preserved – a priority over all else.
- Destroying a life is therefore a heinous crime.
- Abortion is permitted in some circumstances, such as saving the life of the mother.
- Some Jews would also see abortion as allowable in cases of rape, incest, or perhaps even when the general health of the mother was poor.

What do you think?

Is there an answer?

Can religious teaching help – or does it just make it more difficult?

Task

a) Look at each of the points 1–6 in the case study. In pairs, order them to show which would have most importance in making a decision.

b) Write a 'problem page' answer to Sioned for each of the religious traditions you are studying.

What would you advise someone in this situation to do? And what reasons would you give?

ISLAM

- Life is seen to be sacred, and not disposable, except for just causes.
- Allah creates all life, and only he can end it.
- Abortion for purely economic reasons is forbidden in the Qur'an.
- Many do allow abortion if the mother's life is at stake.
- Some will also allow abortion if the child to be born is likely to be seriously deformed or diseased – although others reject this as a just cause.
- The taking of the life of a child is seen as a sin, and in the next life, young children at judgement will have the right to know why they were killed.
- Up to four months after conception the mother's rights are greater than those of the child; after four months the child has equal rights with the mother.
- 120 days after conception 'ensoulment' (receiving of the soul) takes place, therefore some would forbid abortions after this stage.
- There is a purpose in suffering, and no expectation that life will be enjoyable/easy.
- At judgement, Allah will take into account a person's intention (*niyyah*) in the act.

Exam Tip

Many views seem the same. Check out the similarities and differences between the two religious traditions you are studying. Remember to be specific in your answers – do not use a 'cover all' type of answer.

Task

- When you have written your 'problem page' answers from two different religious traditions, list the arguments that are the same, and those that are different from the two religious traditions.

- Make a bulleted list of what you think are the rights of the unborn child. Many people will refer to these when arguing about abortion, so it is good to be aware of them, and use them in your answers. Think of the religious beliefs and teachings that religious believers might link with those rights that you list.

Euthanasia

Whose life is it anyway?

Sometimes, after a terrible accident where people have become paralysed or seriously injured and are in long-term pain, they feel that they no longer want to carry on living. Or perhaps a person has a terminal illness, and is getting progressively worse, and they feel that there might be a time when they will not want to go on living.

Such people feel it is their life, and that they should have a choice whether or not to go on living. They feel that euthanasia should be allowed.

Euthanasia literally means 'gentle death', and is sometimes referred to as 'mercy killing'. It is the speeding up of death, through the use of drugs or other medical ways, to help a person to die. Euthanasia is illegal in Britain, and anyone helping a person to die can be arrested.

There are situations other than the two above where some people think that euthanasia should be allowed:

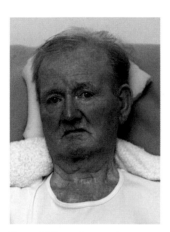

Reginald Crew chose voluntary euthanasia after being crippled and robbed of his dignity by motor neurone disease

- When people are on life-support machines for a long time and there is no real hope of them recovering.

- When a person is in a coma and is not likely to regain consciousness.

- When a person is completely dependent on others for all basic needs.

It is said that there are three different kinds of euthanasia:

Voluntary euthanasia
Where a person has asked someone to help them die. This is not suicide, which is taking one's own life; it is getting help from someone to speed up one's death.

Passive euthanasia
This is allowing someone to die and not taking any steps to prevent the death, or not resuscitating the person after a heart attack or other trauma. It also includes giving a person such high doses of painkillers that they die more quickly, often in less pain.

Non-voluntary euthanasia
This is when the person who dies is not able to make a decision themselves, such as when a life-support machine is switched off.

Is it ever right to end someone's life?

EXIT, otherwise known as the Voluntary Euthanasia Society, is an organisation that has campaigned for the right for people to have the choice to decide about their own death, especially when facing extreme pain, disability or a progressive disease that takes away something of the quality of life.

Part of what they do is provide people with a Medical Emergency Card, which tells doctors what the person's wishes are about being resuscitated or having their life prolonged when there is no likelihood of real independent life.

IN CASE OF EMERGENCY

MEDICAL/OTHER INFORMATION

I do not wish to have CPR, life-support systems, or artificial ventilation. I wish, instead, that distressing symptoms be fully and aggressively controlled by suitable palliative care, ordinary nursing care, analgesic or other treatments; I recognise these may have the effect of shortening my life.

MY NAME IS:

PTO

WWW.EMERGENCYCARDS.CO.UK

IN CASE OF EMERGENCY

The organisation also recommends that people complete a Living Will while alive and well, so that should they ever be in a critical condition or supported mechanically to be alive, the doctors know their personal wishes.

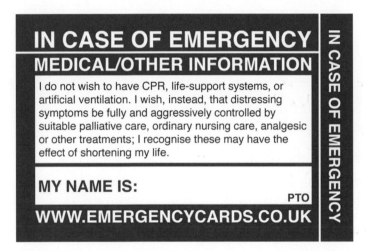

2

Doctors of defiance

Muslim medics say they will refuse to let patients with 'living wills' die

Muslim doctors warned yesterday that they would rather go to jail than allow patients to die in accordance with 'living wills'.

The new Mental Capacity Act allows patients to write the wills, instructing doctors not to try to save them if they become incapacitated. It also allows patients to give 'lasting powers of attorney' to a friend or relative who would be able to instruct doctors to starve to death a patient who becomes incapacitated.

Doctors who refuse to carry out such instructions risk prosecution for assault and a possible jail term.

However, the Islamic Medical Association is urging its members to defy the Act. It fears the law will compel Muslim doctors to stop life-preserving treatment or remove tubes providing food and water. 'All Muslim doctors, nurses and patients, expressing our Islamic beliefs, should oppose this inhumane Act.'

Other religious groups have also voiced their opposition to the law. Earlier this month, the Roman Catholic Church said doctors had a moral obligation to provide food and fluid to patients in a vegetative state.

Anthony Ozimic, of the Society for the Protection of Unborn Children, said the Act placed doctors in a serious dilemma. He urged the Church to support health workers of any faith 'resisting pressure to co-operate in the killing-by-omission of their patients'.

A spokesman for the British Humanist Association said, however: 'The doctor's first duty is to the patient and part of that has to be respecting their patients' deeply held wishes in relation to their care. Doctors' own religious convictions should never be allowed to interfere with patients' rights.'

The British Medical Association has also said it will not support doctors who deliberately ignore patients' wishes.

Daily Mail, 24 September 2007

People who support the EXIT campaign feel that there are good reasons for legalising euthanasia:

- It gives people the chance to die with dignity and peace.

- It ends suffering when there is little chance of improvement.

- It gives people a choice about their lives and their deaths.

- More and more people are living longer, and it may be that in the future the state could not afford to support all those who need it.

- Everyone should have the right to a good quality of life; where that is not possible, they should be able to make a choice to end their suffering.

- Animals are 'put to sleep' when very old, ill or suffering great pain; if it is acceptable for animals, why not people?

- Many doctors would be willing to help people die peacefully, if it were not illegal.

Doctors do recognise that there are times when they can do no more, but they are also anxious that making euthanasia legal not only goes against the Hippocratic Oath, but also puts a lot of responsibility and pressure on them.

Young rugby player paralysed in training chose death over 'second-class' life

Daniel James, aged 23, former England schoolboy rugby player, was injured in a training session in March 2007, and was paralysed from the chest down. Although his paralysis was not terminal, and he had made some progress in regaining the use of his fingers, Daniel was unable to control his hands to any degree and had constant pain in them. He was incontinent and suffered uncontrollable spasms in his legs and upper body. He needed 24-hour care.

It was these things that led Daniel – a very intelligent young man – to repeatedly request death in favour of the kind of life he was leading. Eventually his parents travelled with him to a Dignitas clinic in Switzerland where he was able to undergo an 'assisted suicide'. His parents said: 'His death was an extremely sad loss for his family, friends and all those that cared for him but no doubt a welcome relief from the "prison" he felt his body had become and the day-to-day fear and loathing of his living existence, as a result of which he took his own life.'

Daniel James

Task

- Look at the article on Daniel James the rugby player above and consider his dilemma in the light of all that you have now thought about. What arguments for and against his decision can you identify?

What do religions teach about euthanasia?

Christianity ✝	Buddhism ☸	Hinduism ॐ
Most Christians believe: • in the sanctity of life – so taking any life is wrong • life is a gift from God, and so only he can take it away • death is not the final end, but a 'doorway' to the next life • suffering can have a purpose • there is an alternative in hospices, which offer care and support for the patient and for their family too.	Most Buddhists believe: • taking life is wrong (first of the Five Precepts) • taking a life affects karma • compassion is important, especially in families • dying is an opportunity for spiritual growth • hospices are a good alternative to euthanasia.	Most Hindus believe: • in the principle of ahimsa – not harming any living thing – therefore taking a life is wrong • death is a natural part of life and will come in its time (*kala*) • dharma or duty is important in life, and should be followed through • there may be times when taking a life with purely selfless motives may be acceptable; such as in a 'willed death'.

Islam ☪	Judaism 🕎	Sikhism ☬
Most Muslims believe: • in the sanctity of life, so taking any life is wrong • only Allah can decide when a person dies • suffering has a purpose • it is important to show compassion to those who are in pain or are suffering.	Most Jews believe: • life is the greatest blessing, so should be preserved • life is a gift from God, and God decides when a person's life is to end • in the mitzvah, to practise *pikuakh nefesh* (setting aside some laws in order to save a life).	Most Sikhs believe: • life is a gift from God • the elderly and suffering should be cared for with compassion • suffering should be borne with courage and with grace – it can be a medicine.

IVF (In-vitro fertilisation)

Definition:

The egg of the woman is fertilised outside the womb using either the husband's or a donor's sperm, and then replaced in the womb.

- In some cases an egg is donated by another woman and is fertilised by IVF using the husband's sperm, and then it is inserted into the womb.

- Embryo donation is when both the egg and the sperm come from donors, are fertilised outside of the womb, and then placed inside to allow it to develop and grow.

- For many couples it may be difficult for them to have babies. Up to 10 per cent of couples in the United Kingdom have to get medical help in order to have a baby.

- There are many different examples of solutions produced by medical technology known as Embryo Technology.

Is it right to spend money on IVF?

Many people, when thinking about all the possibilities and dilemmas in medical ethics, begin to question whether it is right to spend vast amounts of money on some medical techniques that are not dealing with life-threatening situations. There are huge problems of starvation, illness and disease in many parts of the world, and many of these could be significantly helped if money was diverted to them from some non-emergency medical expenditure.

It is not an easy question to answer, and the decision people make often depends on whether they or a member of their own family is in need of the medical treatment in question.

Task

- Here is a statement that could appear as an evaluation question:

  'It is morally wrong to spend money on IVF and related medical treatments when there are people starving in the world.'

  Make a list of evidence and arguments to agree with the statement, and a list of those that disagree.

Exam Tip

There are two types of evaluative questions. In (c) questions, for 4 marks, you have to give two reasons from a religious believer's viewpoint, which can be for or against the statement.

In (e) questions, for 8 marks, you must give a range of viewpoints and include reference to religious beliefs.

What do religions teach about IVF?

Christianity

Roman Catholic:
Life is given by God and no one has a right to children. All embryo technology is banned for Catholics because:

- IVF involves throwing away some of the fertilised eggs.
- Children have a right to know who their parents are.
- Fertilisation takes place apart from the sex act, but God intended procreation to be a part of the sex act.
- Pope Pius XII states that third-party IVF is adultery.

Other Christian denominations:
Some would accept the first three bullet points above and would also accept IVF, but wish to point out:

- It provides happiness to the couple.
- Technology is also God's gift, but may be abused.
- Will the cost be justifiable when so many children are starving?

Definition

IVF: Fertilising of the egg outside of the womb.

Buddhism

- There is no infallible authority that a Buddhist has to accept.
- Consideration should be made of the Five Precepts, which state no harm to any living being.

Hinduism

- The Law of Manu encourages infertile couples to adopt a relative.
- IVF is acceptable as they use sperm and egg from husband and wife.
- The discarded embryos are not foetuses as no soul has been transferred to them.
- Embryo donation is not allowed as caste is passed down through the father.

Judaism

- Egg should be donated by a Jewish woman so the child is Jewish.

- Children have a right to know who their parents are.

- Importance of having children is stressed in the tradition.

Islam

- Many accept IVF because the egg and sperm are from the husband and wife.

- It is considered important to know who the natural parents are.

- IVF allowed under special circumstances, such as if a male has a disease.

- The Qur'an warns that the semen or sperm should not be destroyed or wasted.

Sikhism

- Some believe that these areas are likely to involve tampering with the natural body God has given, and are wrong.

- Some believe that using God-given knowledge and skill is important and should be used to help those with disorders.

- IVF (when only the couple's sperm and ovum are used) is acceptable.

Although decisions about medical issues might depend on the particular situations, believers would always consider their beliefs about life, their beliefs about God, and their beliefs about death and any afterlife.

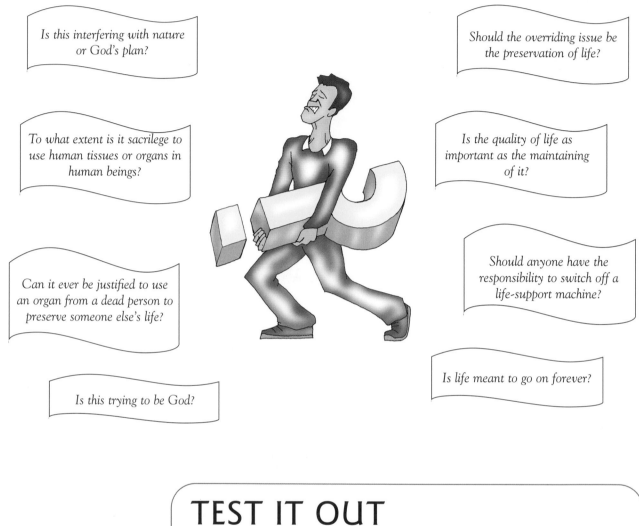

Is this interfering with nature or God's plan?

Should the overriding issue be the preservation of life?

To what extent is it sacrilege to use human tissues or organs in human beings?

Is the quality of life as important as the maintaining of it?

Can it ever be justified to use an organ from a dead person to preserve someone else's life?

Should anyone have the responsibility to switch off a life-support machine?

Is this trying to be God?

Is life meant to go on forever?

TEST IT OUT

(a) *Explain what religious believers mean by 'free will'.* [2]

(b) *Explain how having a religious faith might influence someone making a choice concerning medical ethics.* [4]

(c) *'It's a mother's right to decide about an abortion.' Give **two** reasons why a religious believer might agree or disagree.* [4]

(d) *Explain the teachings of **two** religious traditions about euthanasia.* [6]

(e) *'IVF treatments are unnatural and are trying to be like God.' Do you agree? Give reasons or evidence for your answer, showing that you have thought of more than one point of view. You should include reference to religious beliefs in your answer.* [8]

3 Religious Expression

The Big Picture

Questions to ask

Is pilgrimage out of date?

How can faith be expressed through what is worn?

How can art express one's faith?

Why do people support others?

Can religion give purpose in life?

Does religious faith need to be explicit?

Is there value to interfaith dialogue?

What makes a place conducive to worship?

Can pilgrimage help spiritual growth?

Why worship in special buildings?

How can beliefs drive actions?

Is it right for people to share their faith?

How should the media be used for religious purposes?

What makes a journey special?

Key concepts to think about ▼

COMMUNITY

EVANGELISM

FAITH

IDENTITY

PILGRIMAGE

SACRED

Check it out

The definitions used in the Check it out boxes in this chapter are basic outlines only; always add an appropriate example in your explanation, and remember the context is religious believers.

Religious teachings to explore

- Expressing faith through actions
  - The work of a religious charity or organisation
- Expressing faith through what is worn
- Expressing faith through symbols in a place of worship
  - Purpose and place of symbolism in places of worship
- Expressing faith through pilgrimage
  - Attitudes to pilgrimage
- Expressing faith through sharing faith with others

Ways faith can be expressed

a Through actions to others

b Worshipping in the home

c Worshipping in religious buildings

d Through pilgrimage

e Through symbolism and art

f Through sharing faith with others

g Through what is worn

How can beliefs drive actions?

Check it out

Always add examples

I believe it is important to serve God.

Faith

I believe all humans are created by God.

Believing in the support of someone or something, e.g. God

A belief in a particular religion, e.g. Hinduism

How do religious charities or organisations express their faith?

For most religious believers it is important that they express their beliefs through the way they live their daily life and their actions to others. To help others in need individually or through charities is an important part of expressing faith.

Christianity ✝

Salvation Army

Look it up

http://www.salvationarmy.org.uk

I	dentify	**What is the Salvation Army?** Denomination of the Christian Church.
M	ention	**Which religious tradition does it belong to?** Christianity
P	récis	**What are the main aims?** ● To lead people actively into a saving knowledge of Jesus Christ. ● To actively serve the community irrespective of race, belief, colour, age or sex. ● To fight for social justice.
A	cknowledge	**What are the main aspects of how it is used?** The Salvation Army runs a number of projects to support the homeless, poor, and those in need.
C	onsider	**How does the work demonstrate the teachings of the religion?** Its message is based on the Bible and its motivation is the love of God as revealed in Jesus Christ.
T	ell	**A specific example of a long- or short-term project** It has a team of outreach workers who support the homeless in the streets of towns and cities. They try to build up relationships with the homeless and to offer advice and support. They organise drop-in centres where rough sleepers can get food and warmth.

Christianity ✝

CAFOD

I dentify	**What is CAFOD?** Catholic Fund for Overseas Development.	
M ention	**Which religious tradition does it belong to?** The Roman Catholic denomination of Christianity.	
P récis	**What are the main aims?** ● To educate British Roman Catholics about the need for aid. ● To raise funds to support projects with the poor.	
A cknowledge	**What are the main aspects of how it is used?** It places a great importance on education and awareness raising. Activities will be organised such as 24-hour fasts, Friday Groups where people give up something; and charity shops. It has a disaster fund to deal with natural disasters and refugees in addition to long-term aid.	
C onsider	**How does the work demonstrate the teachings of the religion?** By contributing to the poor and the cause of development, Roman Catholics are acting according to the Gospel tradition.	
T ell	**A specific example of a long- or short-term project** In Brazil there are extremes of wealth and poverty. Many children live on the streets without their family and live a life of abuse and torture. CAFOD is running a scheme called 'The Community Taking Responsibility for its Children' where street children are taught to read and write and get some training to help them find work.	

just one world

Look it up
http://www.cafod.org.uk

CAFOD supports schemes such as Masipag. Masipag is chemical-free farming that uses no chemical fertilisers, pesticides or herbicides

Buddhism ☸

I dentify	**What is Karuna Hospice Services?** A charity that seeks to give holistic care to those with terminal illnesses.	
M ention	**Which religious tradition does it belong to?** A Buddhist based organisation.	
P récis	**What are the main aims?** To give service to people with terminal illnesses in an environment where death, dying and bereavement are openly discussed and accepted.	
A cknowledge	**What are the main aspects of their work?** To give holistic client-centred care, which includes support and counselling for all the family and friends.	
C onsider	**How does the work demonstrate the teachings of the religion?** An important part of the work of the hospice is to openly discuss the impermanence of life. In the Buddha's teachings and actions he showed that all must one day die; it is a natural part of the process. This can be seen in the way that the Buddha helped the mother (Kisagotami) whose child had died (see page 35). *Karuna* (compassion) is an important virtue in Buddhism.	
T ell	**A specific example of a long- or short-term project** An important aspect of the work is giving respite to the carer. This might result in hospice workers taking over duties for a short time such as acting as a caring companion, reading and writing letters, going shopping, so as to give the carer a break from time to time.	

 Look it up

http://www.buddhanet.net/karuna.htm

karuna
HOSPICE **SERVICES**
...a community of compassionate care

Ven. Yeshe Khadro is the Director of Karuna Hospice Services

Hinduism ॐ

I dentify	**What is SEWA?** An organisation and movement established in 1972 in India for poor, self-employed women workers to try to exercise social change.
M ention	**Which religious tradition does it belong to?** Many of its members are Hindu, but the movement has now spread to other countries such as Turkey.
P récis	**What are the main aims?** It's principal aim is to support women to become self-reliant both economically and in decision making. It seeks to organise women workers to obtain work security, income security, food security and social security. The struggle is against the constraints imposed by societies and economies.
A cknowledge	**What are the main aspects of their work?** There are many aspects of the work, which include support for health-care, campaigns for midwives, support for vendors and home-based workers.
C onsider	**How does the work demonstrate the teachings of the religion?** The belief in karma does not mean that there should be a lack of compassion for those who are suffering. It is important to remember that agami karma are the actions that are performed in this life which will affect the future. Gandhian thinking is the principle force of SEWA following the principles of *satya* (truth), *ahimsa* (non-violence), *sarvadharma* (integrating all faiths/people) and *khadi* (promoting local employment and reliance).
T ell	**A specific example of a long- or short-term project** Thousands of women are involved in forest produce collection as their only livelihood. They care for the forest in many ways but do not receive support or technical advice. Instead, forest departments with government support often undercut the women's efforts. SEWA is supporting a project to 'feminise the forests', and involve local nursery bases. Through this way, women will obtain regular incomes.

Look it up

http://www.sewa.org

SEWA vendors

Islam ☾★

I dentify	**What is Islamic Relief?** It is a charity which supports the poorest people in the world.	
M ention	**Which religion does it belong to?** Islam	
P récis	**What is the main aim of the organisation?** To help the suffering of the world's poorest people thorugh long- and short-term aid. It works with all people of all religions and races.	
A cknowledge	**How does Islamic Relief work for justice?** As well as responding to disasters and emergencies it promotes justice through: ● Promoting sustainable livelihoods to ensure people are paid a fair price for their work ● Education for people who are normally too poor to go to school ● Support for health programmes particularly to make people aware of AIDS ● Support for children who have been made orphans.	
C onsider	**How does the work demonstrate the teachings of the religion?** It aims to give immediate relief and also to educate poor people to help crate a more equal world. Their work demonstrates the concept of 'ummah' – community – and teaching from the Qur'an: 'Whoever saved a life, it would be as if he saved the life of all mankind.' (Surah 5:32)	
T ell	**A specific example of a long- or short-term project** When there were serious floods in Gloucester one summer, Islamic Relief workers gave out fresh water to people living in the flooded area, as shown in the photograph below.	

ISLAMIC RELIEF

Look it up
www.islamic-relief.com

Judaism

I dentify	**What is JAT (Jewish Action and Training for sexual health)?** JAT is the only organisation in the UK providing sexual health and HIV awareness programmes for the Jewish community and support for Jewish people living with HIV.
M ention	**Which religious tradition does it belong to?** It belongs to the Jewish tradition and seeks to serve the Jewish community.
P récis	**What are the main aims?** To provide education, counselling and support in connection with HIV/AIDS and sexual health. This includes support and counselling of those affected by HIV/AIDS, as well as awareness-raising work.
A cknowledge	**What are the main aspects of their work?** The primary focus of their work is education and awareness raising in the Jewish community. The trust also offers a completely confidential service which will seek to give support in a number of ways. Counselling is offered not only to those affected by HIV/AIDS, but also to partners, family and friends.
C onsider	**How does the work demonstrate the teachings of the religion?** An important value in Judaism is *bikkur cholim* (caring for the sick), and showing *chesed ve'emet* (loving kindness) not only in thought but also in action. By the educational raising awareness of HIV/AIDS, the trust is exercising *pikuach nefesh* (saving life). Judaism also teaches that every effort should be made to relieve suffering.
T ell	**A specific example of a long- or short-term project** Individual education and aware raising workshops delivered by education volunteers to the Jewish community. The Social Network and the Social Network and Practical Support System (SNAPS) also provides help in meeting the needs of people living with HIV/AIDS. This may include financial support as well as confidential counselling.

Look it up

http://www.jat-uk.org

JAT's primary focus is education and awareness raising

Sikhism

I dentify	**What is Khalsa Aid?** A Sikh organisation working throughout the world.	
M ention	**Which religious tradition does it belong to?** Sikhism	
P rècis	**What are the main aims?** To provide practical relief and service to those suffering.	
A cknowledge	**What are the main aspects of their work?** Serving others in areas of social need.	
C onsider	**How does the work demonstrate the teachings of the religion?** Giving to the hungry is seen as giving to God – but only if it is genuine and from the heart. In the Guru Granth Sahib it says 'the true path to God lies in the service of our fellow beings'. The Sikh emphasis on helping others is seen in the 'langar' – a free communal eating area attached to every gurdwara. In support of the Sikh emphasis on equality Khalsa Aid tries to help all those in need irrespective of caste, creed, gender and religion. Their motto is 'recognising all human beings as one'.	
T ell	**A specific example of a long- or short-term project** Khalsa Aid's first mission was to Albania. They appealed to the *Sangat* (congregation) for food, clothing and money to help the Kosovar refugees. They have been involved in the provision of langar and aid to relieve suffering in the earthquake-torn Gujarat.	

Look it up

http://www.khalsaaid.org

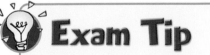

Exam Tip

When you are asked to write about a religious charity or organisation it is important that you read the question carefully and make sure you know what you need to focus on. **In this topic you will be asked to explain how the faith and beliefs of the people are expressed through their actions.**

Khalsa Aid provided relief for earthquake victims in Gujarat

Expressing faith through what is worn

For many believers their faith is expressed through what is worn. Sometimes the clothes may reflect a cultural influence but often they reflect something important about their religion and are an important part of the believer's identity.

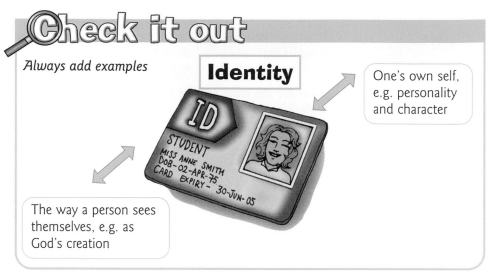

Check it out

Always add examples

Identity

One's own self, e.g. personality and character

The way a person sees themselves, e.g. as God's creation

'Only one of me and nobody can get a photocopy machine.'

James Berry, Jamaican poet

Christianity ✝

Fish sign

'I like to wear a **fish sign**: it reminds me of Jesus, and also tells other people that I am a Christian. It is a symbol used in the times of the persecution of Christians, and came from the Greek word for fish (*icthus*) which makes up a useful summary of my beliefs: Jesus Christ, God's Son, Saviour.'

Crucifix

'My gran gave me my **crucifix** after my confirmation. I always wear it round my neck on a chain. It helps me, especially when I'm worried or upset, and I remember that God is with me wherever I go.'

Vestments

'These **vestments** help to show that the ceremony is a special and important one; it makes me feel humble to be part of such a long tradition; and privileged to be able to lead the ceremony. It is not obligatory to wear them, but I think it helps make Communion holy.'

Salvationist uniform

'Our **uniform** speaks of order and discipline, and reminds everyone of what we stand for: war against evil and suffering; fighting for God and salvation. I am proud to wear it because I am proud of my faith, and of the God I serve.'

Buddhism ☸

No special clothing is worn although members of the **Sangha** (the community of monks and nuns) may wear a robe to show their role within the tradition.

Sikhism ☬

Five Ks

Many male and female Sikhs will wear the Five K's as a symbol of their identity. These are the Kara (bracelet), Kesh (long hair), Kirpan (ceremonial sword), Kachera (shorts) and Kangha (comb). Many Sikh men and some Sikh women will wear a turban. In gurdwaras, worshippers are expected to dress modestly and remove shoes before entering the place of worship. Men and women cover their heads during worship.

Islam ☾☆

Dress

'I decided to wear **hijab** as soon as I started secondary school. It may appear as just a head-scarf but it means so much more to me. It tells me in the Qur'an that it is a way of keeping purity and helps people to see me as I really am – not as a sex symbol. My mother wears the **chador** – this is the black veil to cover almost all her face part from, her eyes. When she was young in Iran, she started to wear it and now she feels uncomfortable if she goes outside without it on. I know she is proud of her chador like I am of my hijab. We both feel it is a part of our religion and identity.'

Judaism

Kippah

'If someone sees my dad and I in the street they can tell right away that we are Jewish because we both wear a **kippah**. When I put it on in the morning I feel that it straight away shows my respect to God by covering that part of my body which is nearest to Him.

Tallit

'My **tallit** was given to me for my Bar Mitzvah, and I know that when I get older I would like to pass it down to my sons, although I know my grandfather was wrapped in his when he was buried. I wear it every morning at prayers. The fringes help remind me of the 613 *mitzvot* or duties that are mentioned in the Torah and are part of the relationship or covenant with God. My sister is of the Liberal Jewish tradition and she has now decided that she too wants to show her religious identity by wearing a kippah and tallit.'

Tefillin

'It took me a while until I could learn to lay **tefillin** properly. These are leather boxes that are tied to the head and upper arm during morning prayers and contain important passages from the Torah. They remind me that I need to serve God with my head and my heart. I feel proud when I wear them because as well as reinforcing my identity as an Orthodox Jew I know I am keeping the duty described in Deuteronomy 6: 8.'

Star of David

'I wear my **Star of David**, or **Magen David**, all the time around my neck. It is not a religious duty to wear it, but I feel it is a mark of my identity as the symbol is often connected with Judaism.

Hinduism ॐ

Tilak mark

'Originally a tilak would be made on the forehead with ash or sandalwood paste but now they can be bought in packs to stick on. My mum wears hers to show she's married, but when I'm going somewhere special then I wear one.'

Airline defends dress policy after check-in worker refused to conceal cross

British Airways is facing legal action and calls for a boycott by Christians after it ruled an employee could not display a cross the size of a five-pence piece on her necklace.

Nadia Eweida, a check-in worker at Heathrow Airport, plans to sue the airline for religious discrimination. BA ruled that Eweida's display of a cross on her necklace breached uniform rules. The airline said items such as hijabs and bangles could be worn 'as it is not practical for staff to conceal them beneath their uniforms'.

A spokesperson added: 'British Airways does recognise that uniformed employees may wish to wear jewellery including religious symbols. Our uniform policy states that these items can be worn, underneath the uniform. There is no ban. This rule applies for all jewellery and religious symbols on chains and is not specific to the Christian cross.'

Eweida said she had just undergone training on respecting and understanding other people's beliefs with BA when she was asked to remove the cross. She said she sought permission to wear it from management, but was refused.

Adapted from the *Guardian*, 15 October 2006

Court says 'Kara-on schooling'

A Sikh teenager who was excluded from school after refusing to take off a religious bangle has won her discrimination case at the High Court. Sarika Watkins-Singh, 14, was reprimanded for breaking the no jewellery rule at Aberdare Girls' School in Wales.

In court, she said wearing the slim steel bracelet was as important to her as it was to cricketer Monty Panesar. Sarika claimed she was the victim of unlawful discrimination when she was first taught in isolation and then excluded. She was the only Sikh among the 600 girls at the school, which does not permit jewellery other than watches and ear studs.

But Justice Silber ruled that the bangle, known as the kara, was a symbol of her Sikh faith and not a piece of jewellery. Silber said that the school was guilty of indirect discrimination under race relations and equality laws.

Eastern Eye, August 2008

Task

- After reading the two news items answer the following question:

  'Religious symbols don't need to be worn to show faith.'

  Give **two** reasons why a religious believer might agree or disagree. [4]

Why worship in special buildings?

For people of a religious faith, one of the ways of expressing their faith is by going to a place of worship.

The purpose of a building is likely to show in the way it is designed. Think about the different purposes between a school and a cinema, and how they are designed to suit their particular purpose.

In the same way, a place designed for worship will have particular requirements and features. Many places of worship include art or calligraphy, which are expressions of the faith of the artist. These in turn help believers in their worship. Look at all the jigsaw pieces below, and decide which would make a place conducive to, or more helpful for worship, and explain how.

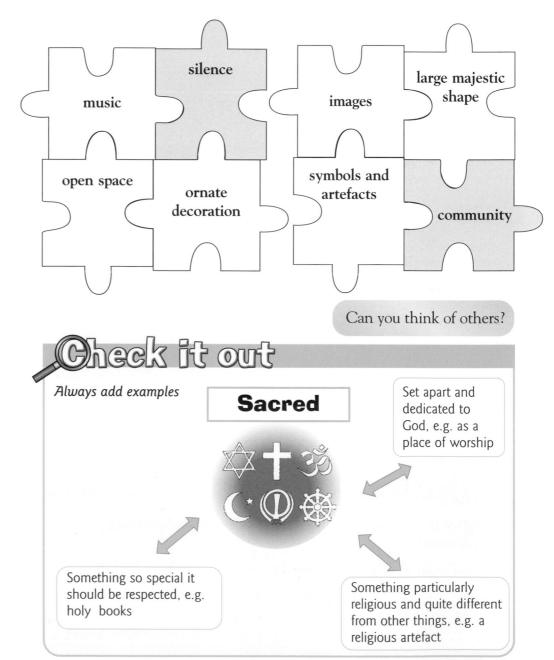

| music | silence | images | large majestic shape |
| open space | ornate decoration | symbols and artefacts | community |

Can you think of others?

Check it out

Always add examples

Sacred

Set apart and dedicated to God, e.g. as a place of worship

Something so special it should be respected, e.g. holy books

Something particularly religious and quite different from other things, e.g. a religious artefact

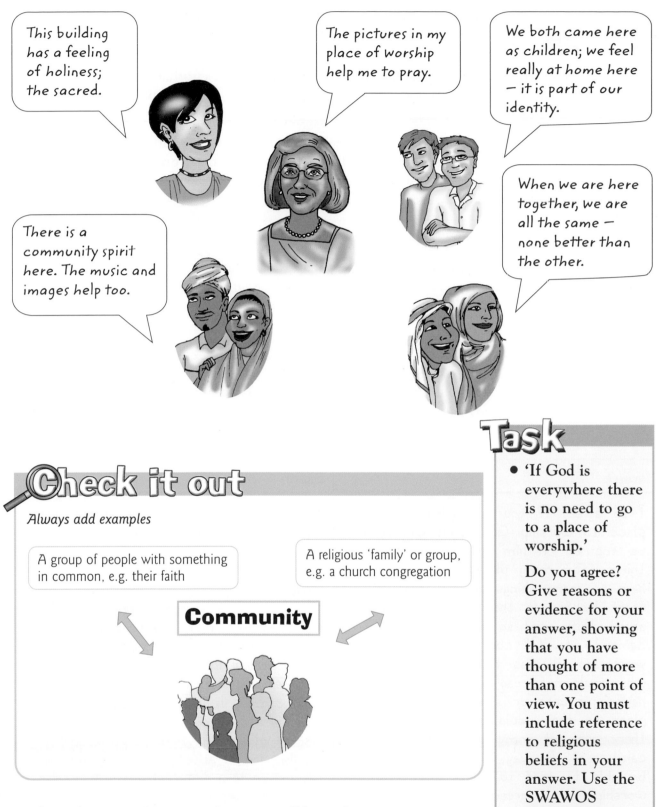

This building has a feeling of holiness; the sacred.

The pictures in my place of worship help me to pray.

We both came here as children; we feel really at home here – it is part of our identity.

There is a community spirit here. The music and images help too.

When we are here together, we are all the same – none better than the other.

Check it out

Always add examples

A group of people with something in common, e.g. their faith

A religious 'family' or group, e.g. a church congregation

Community

Within religious traditions, each person will have their own views on what makes a place conducive to worship. For many people it is important to be part of a community.

Task

- 'If God is everywhere there is no need to go to a place of worship.'

  Do you agree? Give reasons or evidence for your answer, showing that you have thought of more than one point of view. You must include reference to religious beliefs in your answer. Use the SWAWOS framework on page 15 to complete a full answer. [8]

Exam Tip

It is important when answering questions which ask for a point of view, that you express your thoughts clearly and give reasons for what you think, with either good examples or illustrations, or specific religious teaching to support your view.

Many candidates score low levels of marks because they just state a view without comment, explanation or justification. Also remember that you should **show that you have thought about more than one point of view**. So, acknowledge that there are other ideas, which also have reasons and justifications.

Q *'A place of worship should not have lots of images and symbols; it distracts people from worship.' Do you agree? Give reasons or evidence for your answer showing that you have thought about more than one point of view. You must include reference to religious beliefs in your answer.* [8]

Look at the two answers below. Using the Levels of Response Grids on pages 137–38, decide what marks to give to each one. Then, choose one of them, and rewrite it so that it gets full marks.

Answer A	Answer B
I do agree. If you are going to a place to worship God, then you should be focused on him and not on other things. Too many places of worship have so many things around, that you start looking at them and thinking about them, and so forget what you came to do. Of course, many, many years ago, it was thought that people who could not read would be helped by having pictures or symbols around the place so they could understand. But there are not many people today who can't read. Anyway, you don't need to be able to read to think and to worship, so I agree with the statement fully.	I do not agree, as the statement does not take account of the reason for the images and symbols. They have actually been put there to help people in their worship. They help to remind worshippers of important things in their faith, or great stories that come from the sacred writings. These can be a stimulus to thinking and to worship. They can also help in the sense that the place of worship is shown to be special, and set aside for worship; and the quietness, the images and symbols, and the rituals being followed all help to stimulate a sense of worship. Some people disagree, and think this is all very distracting. Well they can just go to a different place of worship where there are no symbols and images – no one makes them go; they should choose what's best for them.

An Anglican church

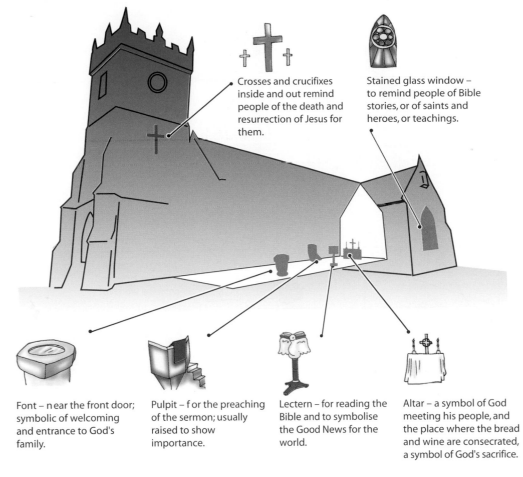

Crosses and crucifixes inside and out remind people of the death and resurrection of Jesus for them.

Stained glass window – to remind people of Bible stories, or of saints and heroes, or teachings.

Font – n ear the front door; symbolic of welcoming and entrance to God's family.

Pulpit – f or the preaching of the sermon; usually raised to show importance.

Lectern – for reading the Bible and to symbolise the Good News for the world.

Altar – a symbol of God meeting his people, and the place where the bread and wine are consecrated, a symbol of God's sacrifice.

Exam Tip

Always be able to explain the purpose of symbols.

Activities and Events:
Sunday Worship: morning, evening (including morning Sunday School)
Regular Midweek: Bible Study/Prayer, Cubs/Brownies, Scouts/Guides, Ladies Group, Young Marrieds, Choir Practice and Music Group
By Arrangement: Baptisms, Confirmations, Weddings, Funerals, special services or private devotions

Some differences

Some churches will have daily services.

Roman Catholic churches will have a tabernacle, stations of the cross, and confessionals.

Chapels are often simpler, but are likely to have a pulpit, a communion table, and a font or baptistry.

An Orthodox church

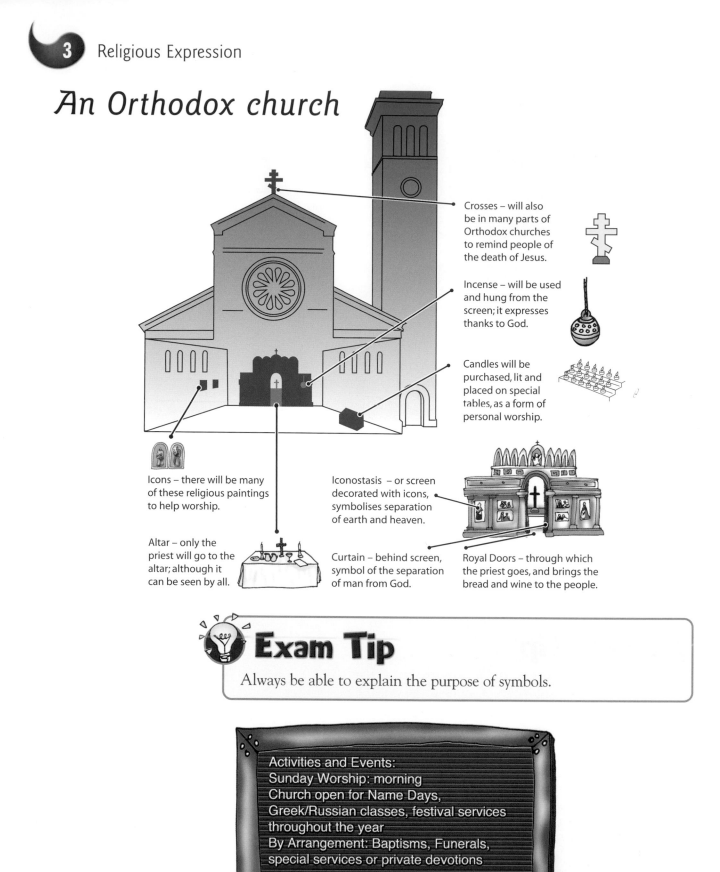

Crosses – will also be in many parts of Orthodox churches to remind people of the death of Jesus.

Incense – will be used and hung from the screen; it expresses thanks to God.

Candles will be purchased, lit and placed on special tables, as a form of personal worship.

Icons – there will be many of these religious paintings to help worship.

Iconostasis – or screen decorated with icons, symbolises separation of earth and heaven.

Altar – only the priest will go to the altar; although it can be seen by all.

Curtain – behind screen, symbol of the separation of man from God.

Royal Doors – through which the priest goes, and brings the bread and wine to the people.

Exam Tip

Always be able to explain the purpose of symbols.

Activities and Events:
Sunday Worship: morning
Church open for Name Days,
Greek/Russian classes, festival services
throughout the year
By Arrangement: Baptisms, Funerals,
special services or private devotions

A Buddhist temple
(e.g. Theravada Tradition)

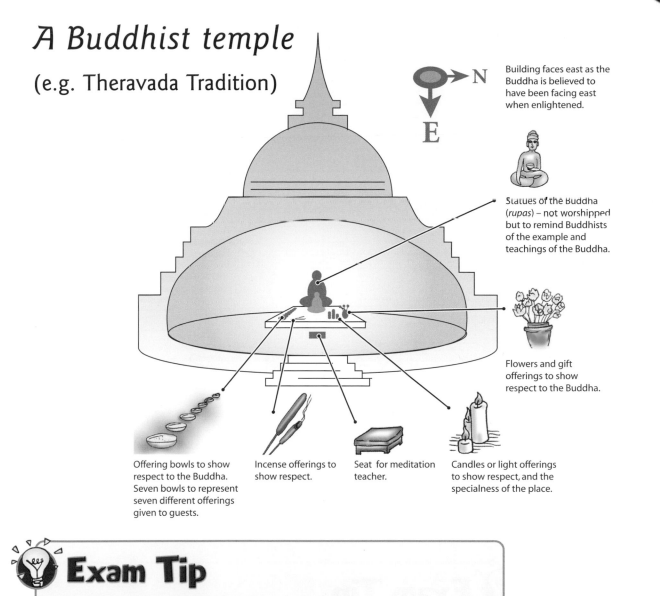

Building faces east as the Buddha is believed to have been facing east when enlightened.

Statues of the Buddha (*rupas*) – not worshipped but to remind Buddhists of the example and teachings of the Buddha.

Flowers and gift offerings to show respect to the Buddha.

Offering bowls to show respect to the Buddha. Seven bowls to represent seven different offerings given to guests.

Incense offerings to show respect.

Seat for meditation teacher.

Candles or light offerings to show respect, and the specialness of the place.

Exam Tip

Always be able to explain the purpose of symbols.

Activities and Events:

Days of retreat and meditation

Festival ceremonies throughout the year

Some differences

Designs of temples differ from country to country, and according to branches of Buddhism. There are many places Buddhists may go to meditate or join in puja. The Mahayanna Buddhists will normally have a central shrine room within the temple campus. Some temple grounds will include a *stupa* (a small monument building containing sacred relics), with a path around it.

A Hindu mandir

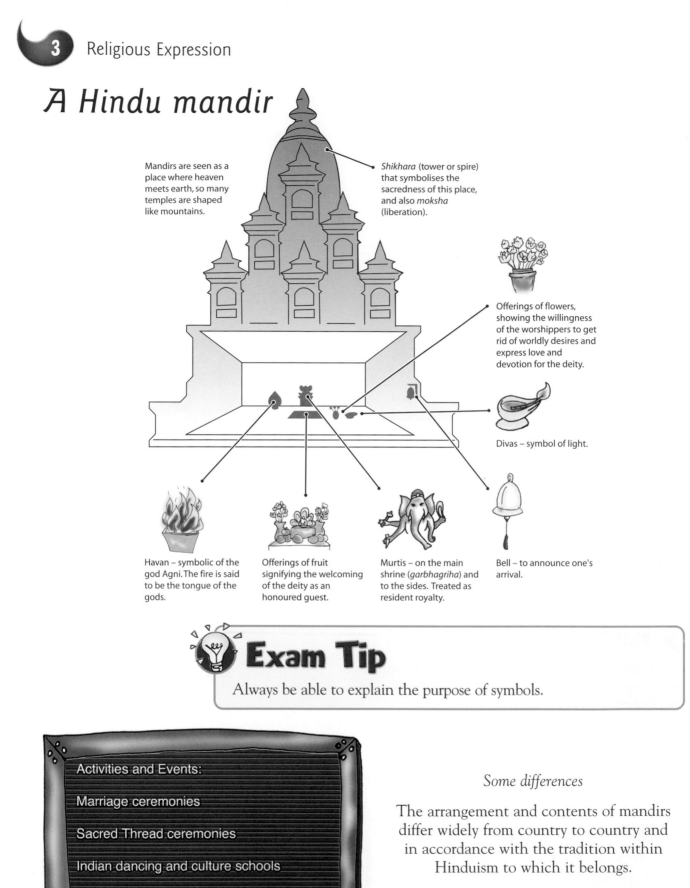

Mandirs are seen as a place where heaven meets earth, so many temples are shaped like mountains.

Shikhara (tower or spire) that symbolises the sacredness of this place, and also *moksha* (liberation).

Offerings of flowers, showing the willingness of the worshippers to get rid of worldly desires and express love and devotion for the deity.

Divas – symbol of light.

Havan – symbolic of the god Agni. The fire is said to be the tongue of the gods.

Offerings of fruit signifying the welcoming of the deity as an honoured guest.

Murtis – on the main shrine (*garbhagriha*) and to the sides. Treated as resident royalty.

Bell – to announce one's arrival.

Exam Tip

Always be able to explain the purpose of symbols.

Activities and Events:

Marriage ceremonies

Sacred Thread ceremonies

Indian dancing and culture schools

Some differences

The arrangement and contents of mandirs differ widely from country to country and in accordance with the tradition within Hinduism to which it belongs.

The home shrine is very important in Hinduism.

A Muslim mosque

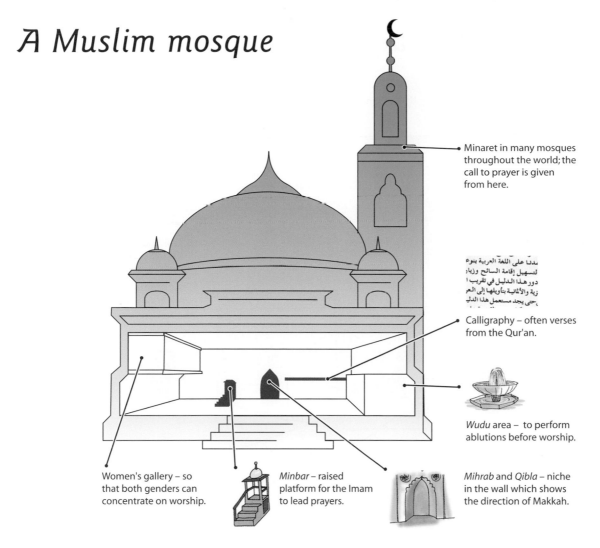

Minaret in many mosques throughout the world; the call to prayer is given from here.

مدنا على اللغة العربية بنوع
لتسهيل إقامة السائح وزيار
دور هذا الدليل في تقريب ا
زية والأمثالية بتأويلها إلى العر
حتى يجد مستعمل هذا الدلي

Calligraphy – often verses from the Qur'an.

Wudu area – to perform ablutions before worship.

Women's gallery – so that both genders can concentrate on worship.

Minbar – raised platform for the Imam to lead prayers.

Mihrab and *Qibla* – niche in the wall which shows the direction of Makkah.

Exam Tip

Always be able to explain the purpose of symbols.

Activities and Events:

Jummah Prayers every Friday

Madrassah school, weekly

By Arrangement: Wedding ceremonies, Funerals, special services or private devotions

A Jewish synagogue

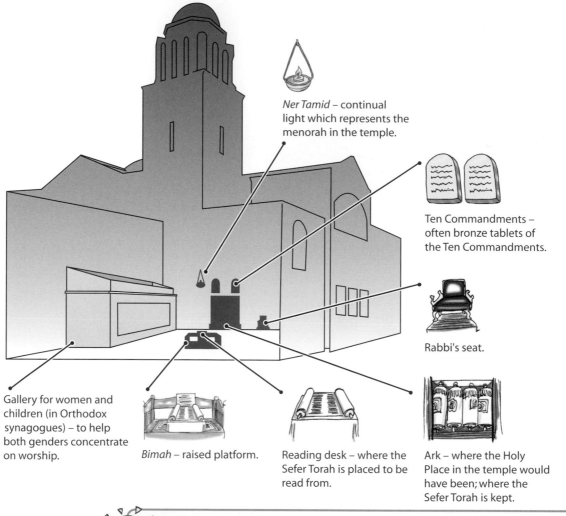

Ner Tamid – continual light which represents the menorah in the temple.

Ten Commandments – often bronze tablets of the Ten Commandments.

Rabbi's seat.

Gallery for women and children (in Orthodox synagogues) – to help both genders concentrate on worship.

Bimah – raised platform.

Reading desk – where the Sefer Torah is placed to be read from.

Ark – where the Holy Place in the temple would have been; where the Sefer Torah is kept.

Exam Tip

Always be able to explain the purpose of symbols.

Activities and Events:

Shabbat service, weekly
Saturday Hebrew school
Service for High Holy Days
By Arrangement: Bar Mitzvah, Bat Chayil, Dedications, Weddings

Some differences

In Reformed synagogues, men and women sit together.

A Sikh gurdwara

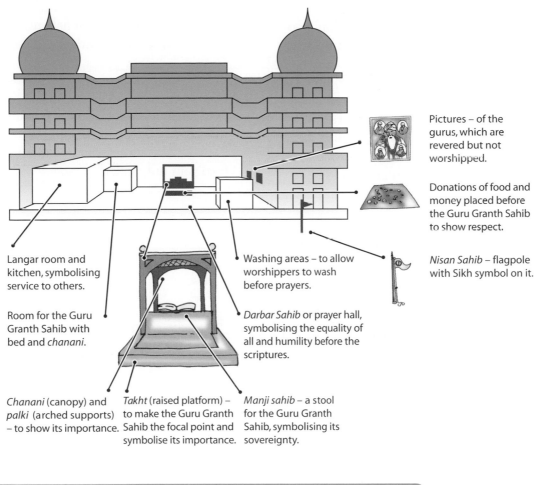

Pictures – of the gurus, which are revered but not worshipped.

Donations of food and money placed before the Guru Granth Sahib to show respect.

Nisan Sahib – flagpole with Sikh symbol on it.

Langar room and kitchen, symbolising service to others.

Room for the Guru Granth Sahib with bed and *chanani*.

Washing areas – to allow worshippers to wash before prayers.

Darbar Sahib or prayer hall, symbolising the equality of all and humility before the scriptures.

Chanani (canopy) and *palki* (arched supports) – to show its importance.

Takht (raised platform) – to make the Guru Granth Sahib the focal point and symbolise its importance.

Manji sahib – a stool for the Guru Granth Sahib, symbolising its sovereignty.

Exam Tip

Always be able to explain the purpose of symbols.

Activities and Events:

Daily Service, Sunday services, Sangrand service, Baisakhi and Divali celebrations, Punjabi classes

By Arrangement: Naming Ceremony, Amrit Ceremony, Weddings, Funerals, Akhand Path service

Some differences

Some gurdwaras do not have pictures of the gurus, as they do not want them to be worshipped or distract from the Guru Granth Sahib.

Exam Tip

This unit is all about religious expression, and so it is important to remember that answers to questions about symbols and symbolism in places of worship, will need to refer to **how they are a way of religious expression, or what effect they have on worshippers and their worship**. Always read the question carefully, and look out for key words – do not just write everything you can about a symbol.

 Q *Explain how **two** examples of religious symbolism within **one** religious tradition help worshippers express their faith and devotion.* [6]

Look at the answer below. Do you think this answer is worthy of six marks? Explain why. How would you improve it to gain full marks?

Name of religious tradition: Christianity

How symbolism helps worshippers: The bread and wine used in some services reminds people of Jesus' death and sacrifice. It helps them to give thanks to God for what he has done for them. Another kind of symbolism used are the stained glass windows, with pictures of the stories in the Gospels, or of famous people in Christianity, like Saints or something. They help worshippers to remember stories and to learn from them. This makes them think more deeply about living out their faith.

Task

- Now write a full answer to the same question for the other religion you are studying.

What makes a journey special?

Check it out

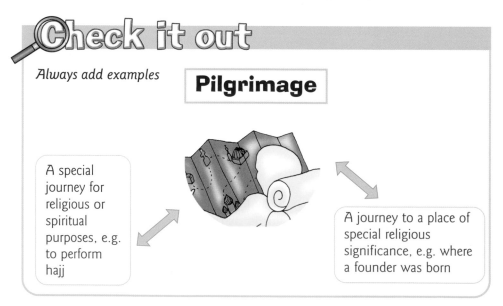

Always add examples

Pilgrimage

A special journey for religious or spiritual purposes, e.g. to perform hajj

A journey to a place of special religious significance, e.g. where a founder was born

All religions have places that are special to members of the faith because of their connections in some way with the founder or important leaders, or where some great happening or experience took place. Often, believers make pilgrimages to such places, to show their devotion, or as a witness to their faith, or to grow spiritually through the experience. Some religions require or expect pilgrimage to be made at some time in one's spiritual life. Others have no requirement, but individual believers, or groups from faith communities, do undertake a pilgrimage as part of their spiritual life and experience. Every day people make special journeys, each of which has its own purpose and destination. Sometimes it is important to go as part of a community. Sometimes it is to be on your own to reflect. Each journey means saving up, leaving friends and family, planning clothes to take, etc.

All religions have their own special journeys, although some are more important than others. For each journey it is as important an inner journey as an outer journey.

'You are older than I am,' said a little fish, 'so can you tell me where to find the ocean?'

'The ocean,' said the older fish, 'is what you are in now.'

'But this is water. What I am wanting is the ocean.'

(adapted from *The Little Fish Story*)

- **Discuss with a partner what this story teaches us about journeys.**

Christianity ✝

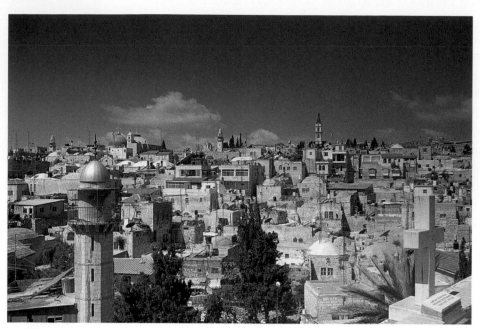

The Holy Land

To walk in the streets where Jesus walked, and to see the places we have so often heard in Bible readings and stories has been absolutely fantastic. The highlight for me was communion in the Garden of Gethsemane. I have never felt anything like it – it was so special. Every communion will be different from now on. Being here and seeing all this and thinking about all that Jesus said and did has made it seem just as if he were here with us. Everyone has felt the same, and some have wept openly as they knelt in prayer. The vicar has been great – I think he has been moved by the way everyone has responded to the visit.

Jonathan

There is no requirement for Christians to go on any pilgrimage, but many Christians wish to visit the Holy Land, and specific sites within it, because of its connections with Jesus and his life.

The Church of the Nativity at Bethlehem, Golgotha (the place where Jesus was crucified) and the Garden tomb in Jerusalem are the most popular sites.

Many pilgrims like to walk along the Via Dolorosa (the path Jesus walked from Pilate to Golgotha), and often will stop and meditate and pray, or listen to the readings of the New Testament about the events.

Find out about another place of Christian pilgrimage.

Look it up
www.travelinkuk.com

Christianity ✝

Lourdes

I didn't really want to come here because I wasn't sure that it would make any difference to my condition. But it has been truly amazing. Although medically I am no different, I *feel* so different. Stronger somehow, and more able to cope with my illness. And the love that has been shown here, and the sense of God's love is so overwhelming. Isn't it wonderful that so much can happen in a place such as this. Thank you for encouraging me to come!

Molly

One of the most popular Christian pilgrimage sites is Lourdes, in France, where St Bernadette is said to have had a number of visions of the Virgin Mary. There is a spring of water there that is claimed to have healing properties, and many pilgrims go because of illness or disease. Since 1873 there have been about 64 cases declared as miracles, but many people have felt greatly helped by visiting the place because:

- They have felt a real sense of God's presence
- They feel spiritually refreshed and encouraged
- They have a greater sense of community and identity through the experience.

Find out about another place of Christian pilgrimage.

Look it up

http://re-xs.ucsm.ac.uk/re/
pilgrimage/
www.request.org.uk/
main/dowhat/pilgrimage/
pilgrim01.htm

Buddhism ☸

Bodh Gaya and Kapilavastu

To all at Cardiff Road Temple.

Can you see the Bodhi tree? This grew from the seed of the same tree that Buddha sat under when he was meditating. Like the other pilgrims, I walked round the tree and sat under it to meditate. Most of the pilgrims had bare feet and heads, to show their respect. I am so glad I came, it has been really inspiring! I feel that all the meditations and readings we have done back home have suddenly all come together.

Joanna

Buddhists try to make pilgrimages to the principal locations in the life of the Buddha, like Bodh Gaya, where he gained enlightenment, and Kapilavastu, where he was born.

For some Buddhists pilgrimage is believed to:

- Bring about religious merit
- Be inspirational
- Re-affirm religious practices.

Find out about another place of Buddhist pilgrimage.

Look it up

http://www.buddhanet.net

Hinduism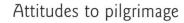

Ganges/Varanasi and Allahabad

Since coming to Varanasi I just feel so different. It is so hard to believe that here I am at the foremost city of Shiva. There are so many reasons why people are here. Some have come in the hope of finding liberation, some to accompany the cremation ghats, and many like to participate in worship at the holy places. Wherever I go there are people taking guidance and listening to talks. I have walked around many temples, and tried to get as near to the Ganges to bathe. So much to think about – so much to do!

Sejal

For Hindus, a special place to die or be cremated is preferred, as this helps give good karma.

Pilgrims travel with a purpose, meditate and reflect.

They hope for spiritual fulfilment. There are about 2000 temples in this region.

Find out about another place of Hindu pilgrimage.

Look it up

http://www.hindunet.org

95

Islam ☪

Makkah

Wow! Being here is much more exciting and fantastic than I expected – and I did expect it too! There are thousands of people, but we are all the same – all of one mind and purpose. Wearing the ihram is so special too; I really feel different, and just caught up in all the holiness and spirituality around here. Seeing the Kaaba, and circling it, was quite incredible.

Really looking forward to going to Mina on 10 Dhul Hijja. Tell you all about it when I get back!

Ahmed

For Muslims, the Hajj to Makkah is one of the five duties or pillars expected, provided they are healthy and can manage to pay for the journey.

Special dress for men, called *ihram*, is worn – two unsewn pieces of cloth, one tied round the waist, the other thrown over the shoulder. It is a symbol of holiness and purity, humility and equality, and dedication.

Find out about another place of Muslim pilgrimage.

Look it up

http://www.islam.org/hajj

Judaism

Israel and the Western Wall

I wish you could have come to my Bar Mitzvah in Jerusalem. It was so special going through the ceremony after having been to the Western Wall. I don't think I have ever felt so moved! It has made me really proud to be Jewish, and really determined to live the faith. In a way I suppose that's what Bar Mitzvah is – but I'm so glad we were able to do it here in Israel.

We've taken loads of photographs, and a video of the Bar Mitzvah itself, so you'll see it all when we get back.

Benjamin

According to the Torah all Jews should go to Jerusalem for the three Pilgrim festivals – Passover; Shavuot; Sukkot. After the destruction of the Temple many would go to the ruins of the Western Wall to mourn its destruction. Since the reunification of Israel in 1967 many Jews have considered it important to visit Israel and in particular the Western Wall in Jerusalem and Masada. Many Jews consider it important to visit graves of important spiritual rabbis and scholars.

Find out about another place of Jewish pilgrimage.

Look it up

http://www.virtualjerusalem.com

Sikhism

Amritsar and the Golden Temple

Can't believe I'm here in this great historic city. To think that Guru Nanak once meditated here. Went in to the Golden Temple which was begun to be built by Guru Ram Das in 1573. It is in the middle of a lake, with four doors around it to show people from all parts of the world are welcome. And there are so many people from all over the world! It's so special being here, and realising that this place has been a place of pilgrimage for so long – amidst all the activity, you can just feel the spirituality.

Kanwaljit

Pilgrimage is not a religious duty for Sikhs, but many choose to go for historic reasons to see the places associated with Amritsar and the Golden Temple.

As with other religions, the benefits are seen to be in the increase of spirituality, the demonstration of one's faith to others, and the sense of connection to the past and long standing tradition from which one's religion and its practices come.

Find out about another place of Sikh pilgrimage.

Look it up

http://www.sikhnet.com

Is pilgrimage out of date?

Sometimes questions are raised about the historical accuracy of events that were supposed to have happened at sacred sites. It must be remembered, however, the purpose of going on pilgrimage is not so much factual or historical, as spiritual.

Q CASE STUDY
Helen has to complete an evaluation for her RE homework. The question is: *'Pilgrimage has no relevance any more.' Do you agree? Give reasons or evidence for your answer showing that you have thought of more than one point of view. You must include reference to religious beliefs in your answer.* [8]

These are the points of view Helen has found out:

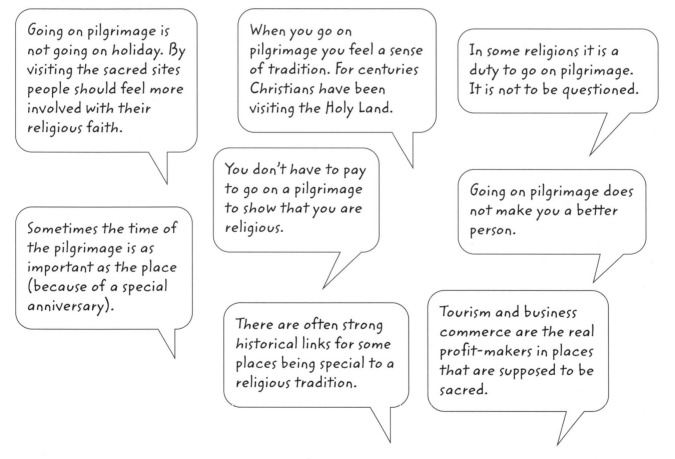

Going on pilgrimage is not going on holiday. By visiting the sacred sites people should feel more involved with their religious faith.

When you go on pilgrimage you feel a sense of tradition. For centuries Christians have been visiting the Holy Land.

In some religions it is a duty to go on pilgrimage. It is not to be questioned.

You don't have to pay to go on a pilgrimage to show that you are religious.

Going on pilgrimage does not make you a better person.

Sometimes the time of the pilgrimage is as important as the place (because of a special anniversary).

There are often strong historical links for some places being special to a religious tradition.

Tourism and business commerce are the real profit-makers in places that are supposed to be sacred.

Can you add any more views or ideas yourself?

Task

- Now complete Helen's evaluation question, using the SWAWOS framework (see page 15). In your answer you must include the following key terms: duty; faith; community; sacred; identity.

Which four points would you choose, and what extra information would you give to each?

Sharing faith with others

Interfaith activity
group

Evangelistic crusade

Media broadcasts

Literature Tracts

Other ways of sharing faith:
Collective worship in schools
Working together after disaster or tragedy
Prison visiting
Council of Faith in cities

When is sharing one's faith:

Raising awareness	
Creating harmony	**?**
Unacceptable intrusion	

Evangelism

Within some religions, there is an expectation or an emphasis on making an effort to tell other people about the faith. This may take many forms, such as giving out pamphlets (often called 'tracts'), holding special 'evangelistic' services or missions, making door-to-door visits in a particular neighbourhood, or simply individuals telling their friends and neighbours about their beliefs, and inviting them to join them at events in their place of worship.

Mission

Mission is a word that means 'the act of sending', or, 'the duty on which a person is sent'. So in religion it refers to the act of going out to preach the faith to others – because the person (or missionary) is sent.

Evangelism

'Evangel' is a word meaning 'good tidings' or 'the Gospel'. So evangelism has come to mean the ways and means some religions take to spread their beliefs to others. A person engaged in this sort of work would be called 'an evangelist'.

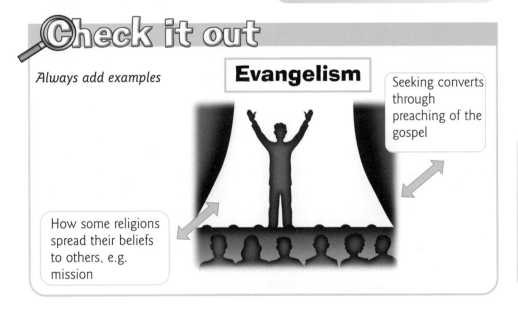

Check it out

Always add examples

Evangelism

How some religions spread their beliefs to others, e.g. mission

Seeking converts through preaching of the gospel

Conversion

This is a term meaning a change from one religion to another, or from no religion to being a religious person.

Within some religious traditions, attitudes to mission and evangelism vary greatly. Some branches of Christianity – those sometimes referred to as 'evangelical' or 'evangelistic' – feel that telling others about the faith, so as to lead to 'conversion', is an important task and duty of the Christian. They believe it is what Jesus commissioned them to do. Others feel that it is right and proper to be open about one's faith, and even to share it with others, but that people need to make their own personal choices about what to believe.

As far as most other religions are concerned, there is always a willingness to share faith with others, and a willingness to accept those who do convert to the religion from elsewhere. However, there is less emphasis on mission and evangelism as described above.

Sharing one's faith

Whenever people believe in something, and it is important to them and their way of life, they inevitably like to talk about it with others. Sometimes this will be with others who share the same beliefs, or it may be to tell others who don't share that belief, as described above. Many people share their faith with others in order to promote a mutual understanding.

Tom and Leanne are studying GCSE RS.

Tom: I saw in the newspaper that there is an interfaith meeting tonight and they are discussing the importance of pilgrimage in three different faiths.

Leanne: So?

Tom: So it would help us with our GCSE. It's one of the areas we need to know.

Leanne: I'm not going to that – they will just want to convert me!

Tom: No they won't. It's where people from different faiths share their beliefs. It isn't an evangelistic meeting.

Leanne: What do you mean?

Tom: That it's not a meeting where people are going to want you to join them in their religion. It's to explore common grounds between different faith groups.

Leanne: Hey, I have enough of them knocking at my door trying to convert me. I'm not going to spend my evening there!

Tom: Have you ever thought that people who do knock at your door are doing that because they want to share their good news with you? They believe it is what Jesus wants them to do.

Leanne: Well, I get fed up with it! It's like when you switch on the TV and all those stations just talking about religion. They've always got dodgy hair styles as well!!! TV should be for entertainment.

Tom: Many people get great comfort from listening to religious programmes on TV. Some people can't get to a place of worship and it's a great comfort for them. Doesn't your TV have an off switch?

Leanne: I tell you what. You go to the meeting tonight and take some notes for me and I'll swap you the notes I make when I interview Farhana to find out why she wants to wear hijab.

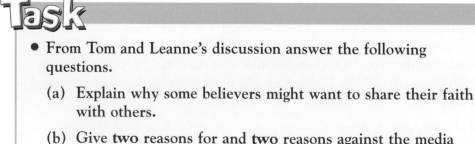

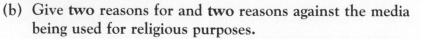**Task**

- **From Tom and Leanne's discussion answer the following questions.**

  (a) **Explain why some believers might want to share their faith with others.**

  (b) **Give two reasons for and two reasons against the media being used for religious purposes.**

Sharing one's faith with others

As mentioned in the section on evangelism, there are differing attitudes within religious traditions regarding sharing one's faith.

Hinduism

'God's grace is like a strong wind that's always blowing. But we have to raise our own sails.'

Ramakrishna (1834–1886) A Brahmin who believed that God is present in every religion

'No peace among the nations without peace among the religions;
no peace among the religions without dialogue between the religions.'

Hans Kung

Sikhism

'The founder of our religion, Guru Nanak, said in his very first sermon that "There is neither Hindu nor Muslim." What he meant by that was not that Hindus and Muslims, or for that matter Sikhs, Christians, Jews and other faiths, do not exist. Rather, he meant that God does not look at religious labels but at how we live and how we act. To follow on from that teaching, Guru Arjan, the fifth Guru, in compiling the Guru Granth Sahib, also included verses by Hindus and Muslims in our holy books in order to show respect of other religions. He also asked a Muslim holy man to lay the foundation stone of the Golden Temple to show this respect for other religions. Then the ninth Guru, Guru Tegh Bahadur, gave his life defending the right of those of another religion to worship in the manner of their choice.'

Indarjit Singh

Buddhism

'I have for many years now engaged in interfaith dialogue and understanding with the basic belief that many major religions of the world have the same potential to transform people into better human beings. The common messages of love, kindness, tolerance, self-discipline and a sense of sharing are in some ways the foundation for respecting the fundamental and basic human rights of every person. The world religions therefore contribute to peace, harmony and human dignity.'

Dalai Lama

Christianity

'There are Christians who see "dialogue" as a way to convert others. They point to Jesus saying, "No one comes to the Father except through me" (John 14:6). Others hope that dialogue will create a new unified understanding of God, as the reality that underlies all religions.

'Other Christians see dialogue as a way of promoting peace and justice, through understanding and mutual respect. They point to Jesus' debate with a foreign woman (Mark 7:24–30), and his use of the Samaritan as a caring neighbour (Luke 10: 25–37), as examples of being open to others. This approach expects both partners in the dialogue to contribute something, to learn from each other, and to be changed by the process.'

Rev Simon Walkling, United Reformed Church Minister, South Wales

Islam

'People need to learn more about their neighbours so that ignorance doesn't breed more fanaticism.'

Yusuf Islam

Look it up

www.uri.org.uk
(United Religions Initiative)

www.interfaith.org.uk
(Inter Faith Network for the UK)

Judaism

'One of the greatest achievements of the second half of the twentieth century is that this previously troubled relationship (between faiths), the cause of so much pain and suffering has begun to be healed, and in the process new hope has been given to humanity.'

Dr Jonathan Sacks, Chief Rabbi of Great Britain and the Commonwealth

Exam Tip

In an exam you will need to relate to a range of topic content. It is important you select appropriate examples.

Task

- Look back over the work in this topic and make a list of the positive and negative points that can be given in answer to the question 'Can a religion give a purpose in life?'

Can a religion give a purpose in life?	
Yes, because ●	No, because ●

- Select appropriate examples of content you would use to answer the following questions:
  - Why do people support each other?
  - How can beliefs drive actions?

TEST IT OUT

(a) Explain what religious believers mean by 'faith'.   [2]

(b) Explain how having a religious faith might encourage believers to go on pilgrimage.   [4]

(c) 'Religious believers should not be allowed to wear symbols of their faith.' Give **two** reasons why a religious believer might agree or disagree.   [4]

(d) Explain how faith is expressed through the work of two religious charities or organisations. (You must state the religious traditions you are referring to.)   [6]

(e) 'Your religion is your own business. You shouldn't talk about it to anyone.' Do you agree? Give reasons or evidence for your answer, showing that you have thought about more than one point of view. You must include reference to religious beliefs in your answer.   [8]

4 Authority – Religion and State

The Big Picture

Questions to ask

How should we deal with offenders?

How and why do people get justice for others?

Should we obey authority? What if authority is wrong or conflicts with religious belief?

How do we know our duties?

Should everyone have the same human rights?

How can human rights be maintained?

Is it ever right to take a life?

What influence can sacred texts have and how far should people follow them?

Key concepts to think about ▼

AUTHORITY

DUTY

JUSTICE

HUMAN RIGHTS

PERSONAL CONVICTION

PUNISHMENT

Religious teachings to explore

- Human rights
  – An example of a religious believer who has worked for human rights
- Duty
- Punishment
  – The aims and purpose of punishment
- Capital punishment
- The role of sacred texts in individuals' lives
  – Holy texts/Sacred books as a source of authority
- Examples of conflict between personal conviction and authority (religious, state and social)

Check it out

The definitions used in the Check it out boxes in this chapter are basic outlines only; always add an appropriate example in your explanation, and remember the context is religious believers.

105

Why should we obey authority?

Religious leaders

Judges and courts

Conscience

Police

Forms of Authority

Government

Teachers

Written laws

Sacred texts

Check it out

Always add examples

Authority

Right or power over others

The moral power behind a person's words or actions, e.g. conscience

The law or those who ensure it is kept/enforced, e.g. religious rules or leaders

Task

• What other forms of authority do you have in your life?

Why should we obey authority?

> I don't want to get punished!

> My parents are better judges of what I should do so I need to obey them.

> It's against my conscience to disobey what the law says I should do.

> It's my duty to obey my parents.

> I don't want to get punished.

> My holy books tell me how to behave. It is the word of God.

Duty

Check it out

Always add examples

Duty

Something a person is expected to do, or be, because:

– it is the law or part of a contract

– it is the accepted pattern of behaviour or action

– of conscience or religious beliefs

– it is expected as a result of one's job or responsibility

The duty we should keep depends on the country, family and religious group to which we belong.

Duty is something a person is expected to do or be because:

- it is part of the law or part of a contract
- of conscience or religious beliefs
- it is the accepted pattern of behaviour or action
- it is expected as a result of one's job or responsibility.

Therefore duty is something that results in action – it is not just a feeling or an awareness – but it is an action that the person feels they must carry out, even if doing so may seem to go against self-interest.

For many religious believers, seeking justice for others is an important religious duty.

Check it out

Always add examples

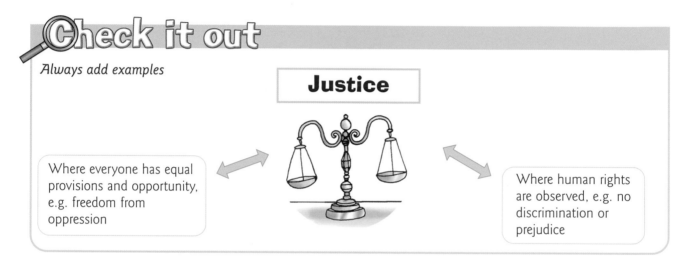

Justice

Where everyone has equal provisions and opportunity, e.g. freedom from oppression

Where human rights are observed, e.g. no discrimination or prejudice

This is the duty of our generation as we enter the twenty-first century —solidarity with the weak, the persecuted, the lonely, the sick, and those in despair.

Elie Wiesel, a Jewish writer and Holocaust survivor

Task

- You are a worker for a marketing company and have been asked to produce a picture or collage to explain the quote above.

 Exam Tip

In the exam you are asked to respond to quotes by people. Make sure that you understand the whole of it. The quote from Elie Wiesel refers not only to the weak and persecuted but the fact that we should enter in solidarity with them.

Religious teachings about duty

Christianity ✝

For most Christians, duty is related to:

- loving God, or Christ, with all of one's heart, soul, mind and strength
- loving one's neighbour as oneself.

This was Jesus' summary of the Ten Commandments, and it has become a general guideline for everyday living. It also includes action to seek justice for others.

Buddhism ☸

The main duty for Buddhists is Sila, which is keeping the precepts of behaviour. There are several levels of Sila:

- the Five Precepts (or basic morality)
- the Ten Precepts (for novice monks)
- Vinaya, or Pratimokkha (for monks).

The Five Precepts are training rules that help people to live better lives:

To refrain from taking life.
To refrain from taking what is not given.
To refrain from sensual misconduct.

To refrain from lying.
To refrain from intoxicants which cloud the mind.

Keeping these precepts is not only a duty, but they help to promote the peace of mind of the person as well as peace in the community.

Hinduism ॐ

Dharma or duty is an important aim, and is one of the four ends or aims in life in Hinduism. It is really about moral living, and includes *ahimsa* (not harming any living things) and *satya* (seeking the truth). Dharma is the second highest aim; the lower two are *kama* (sensual pleasure) and *artha* (wealth or prosperity). The highest is *moksha* (liberation), which is what performing one's duty is designed to achieve.

For many Hindus, their dharma or duty depends on their age and position in life. For example, it is a duty of students to learn well at school and respect parents and grandparents.

Islam ☾

All Muslims are required to keep the Five Pillars of Islam. These are the five duties that unite all Muslims throughout the world.

The Five Pillars	**Focuses on**
Shahadah	Belief – recited many times each day
Salah	Prayer – five times a day
Zakah	Giving – normally 2.5% of wealth each year
Sawm	Fasting – during the month of Ramadan
Hajj	Pilgrimage – journey to Makkah

In addition to these five duties, Muslims also have *Shari'ah* or Islamic laws that cover all aspects of living. The word 'Shari'ah' literally means 'straight path', and Muslims see following these laws as a duty because it leads to the best kind of life.

Judaism ♈

For Jews, the main duty in life is keeping the *mitzvot*, or commandments, that are contained in the Torah. Traditionally there are 613 mitzvot, which are divided into 'positive commandments' – actions that should be performed (*mitzvoit aseh*), and 'negative commandments' – actions to be avoided (*mitzvoth lo taaseh*). These include the Ten Commandments.

However, it is a duty that all people, regardless of their wealth or status, should perform *tzedakah* – charitable or humanitarian acts.

Sikhism ☬

Guru Nanak taught that all Sikhs should ensure that their lives contained three important aspects:

- *Naam Japna* – or engaging in daily meditation, reciting and chanting God's name, repeating spiritual songs aloud or silently. These things can be done throughout one's waking hours.
- *Kirat Karni* – living honestly and earning a living through one's physical and mental efforts.
- *Vand Chakna* – sharing one's wealth within the community and outside it, by giving a tenth of one's wealth (*Dasvand*) and practising *Sewa* or service to others – selfless service. This can be done in the gurdwara, in the local community, in people's homes, in care centres, or when there are disasters or emergencies of some kind.

- **Design a simple poster or web chart to show the main points of the teachings on duty of the religious traditions you have studied.**

Aims and purposes of punishment

Check it out

Punishment

To inflict a penalty on a person, e.g. penance

To make a person suffer pain or loss for a wrongdoing, e.g. prison or a fine

Although many religious believers feel it is important to help offenders recognise the wrong they have done and to try and support them, many religions have very definite viewpoints concerning capital punishment because the taking of any life interferes with the belief in sanctity of a God-given life.

Retribution
A form of revenge on behalf of those who were wronged or subject to attack.

Reparation
Criminals should have the right to 'pay' for the wrong they have done – to show they are sorry and 'repair' the damage done.

Reform
Trying to ensure the criminal is helped to change their approach and way of life.

Protection
Making sure that all people, and society itself, is kept free from possible recurring of a crime by a criminal; criminals themselves also need protection.

Vindication
To show that the law and authority are of supreme importance; and ensure that the law is upheld, and justified.

Deterrence
To try to deter (or discourage) people from committing crimes, because they know what the punishment is, and know it will be given to those caught committing a crime.

Capital punishment

Capital punishment is when a person is put to death as a punishment for a crime. Sometimes it is referred to as 'the death penalty'. In the United Kingdom the death penalty for murder was abolished in 1969.

JON: Did you see that film last night, with the execution? He got just what he deserved!

SARAH: You are so sad! It was horrible. How can anyone enjoy watching someone else be tortured and die?

JON: He wasn't being tortured. He was put in the electric chair because he had murdered someone else. He got what he deserved.

SARAH: But it's a life taken away, isn't it? Surely the person who took his life away is a murderer too?

JON: They were doing a duty to other human beings. That man could have escaped prison and gone out and murdered again. With his execution it will make other people think before taking someone's life.

SARAH: So you've got proof that capital punishment is a deterrent then?

JON: What do you want? Should he be kept on Death Row for the rest of his life? Have you any idea how much it costs to keep people in prison? All that money could be spent on schools and hospitals.

SARAH: But what about those people who are wrongly accused? Mistakes happen. There's no point saying sorry after they are dead.

JON: But those are one-offs. Society needs to be protected from cold-blooded murderers.

SARAH: So you would say that two wrongs make a right!! Have you any idea what people are executed for throughout the world? Many people are executed for crimes such as prostitution, practising a religion or speaking out against a government. Look on the Amnesty website and you'll see what I'm talking about.

Look it up

http://www.amnesty.org

Task

- **From the dialogue between Sarah and Jon above, make a list of the arguments for and against capital punishment.**

Christianity ✝

How do Christians treat people who break the laws?
What do Christians teach about capital punishment?

Christians would turn to the Bible for support and guidance. One passage that would be important for this issue would be:

> 'Repay no one evil for evil, but take thought for what is noble in the sight of all. If possible, so far as it depends upon you, live peaceably with all. Beloved, never avenge yourselves, but leave it to the wrath of God; for it is written, "Vengeance is mine, I will repay, says the Lord." No, "if your enemy is hungry, feed him; if he is thirsty, give him a drink; for by so doing you will heap burning coals upon his head." Do not be overcome by evil, but overcome evil with good.'
>
> Romans 12: 17–21

Christianity is a religion of forgiveness. It teaches that by following the example of Jesus, people are forgiven by God, and so believers should act in a similar manner and forgive others.

This does not mean liking the person. When Pope John Paul II survived an assassination, he asked for mercy for the person who had tried to kill him.

However, some Christians would also argue that although it is good to forgive someone for a wrong they have done, and give them a new start, there is also the idea of justice, and that means that there should be a punishment. They would say that punishment and forgiveness can – and should – go together.

Generally:
- Christians often have personal considerations on this issue
- Reference to the commandment 'Thou shalt not kill'
- All life is sacred
- Jesus taught compassion not revenge
- The Old Testament says 'an eye for an eye'

SOCIETY OF FRIENDS (Quakers):
- Have campaigned against capital punishment since 1818
- Reverence for all is important
- Punishments should be used to reform

Buddhism ☸

How do Buddhists treat people who break the laws?
What do Buddhists teach about capital punishment?

In Buddhism the root of evil is ignorance and delusion. A sinful or wrong act (pap) produces bad karma which might result in rebirth in the hell states.

Buddhist countries do have a system of punishment as there is a fear that there would be more violence without a system. Many Buddhists disagree with the concept of retribution as they say this is opposed to the teaching of metta (loving kindness) and karuna (compassion). This is particularly the argument against capital punishment, although some Buddhists argue for alternatives that are non-violent.

> 'As sweet as honey is an evil deed, so thinks the fool so long as it ripens not; but when it ripens, then he comes to grief.'
>
> Dhammapada 69, 71

- Buddhists argue about its appropriateness in deterring crimes
- The First Precept deplores the taking of life
- Buddhism acknowledges that it depends on state law
- It is against the Buddhist principle of metta (loving kindness)
- It is also against the principle of karuna (compassion)

Hinduism ॐ

How do Hindus treat people who break the laws?
What do Hindus teach about capital punishment?

Any form of sin is an act against dharma (duty). For the Hindu their dharma includes self-control, religious and social duty, rules and customs in religious ceremonies and worship, good conduct, and their keeping to the law.

The rules for varnashramadharma are contained in the holy texts and there are punishments or danda. This includes retribution, restraint and reformation.

> 'Perform your prescribed duty, which is better than not working. Whoever does not work will not succeed even in keeping his body in good repair.'
>
> Bhagavad Gita 3:8

The Laws of Manu give lists of actions that are crimes and what the punishments should be. They also say that people who are never caught for their crimes will be punished because their bad actions will bring about bad karma in the present or future life.

- It is against the principle of ahimsa
- Used to depend on caste
- Individuals are likely to suffer for their wrongdoing in this life or the next

Islam ☪

How do Muslims treat people who break the laws?
What do Muslims teach about capital punishment?

'The good deed and the evil deed cannot be equal. Repel the evil deed with one which is better, then he who was your enemy will become like a close friend.'

Surah 41:34

'The reward for an injury is an equal injury in return, but whoever forgives and makes reconciliation, his reward is due from Allah.'

Surah 42:40

Within Islam forgiveness and reconciliation are very important but so also is the need to protect the whole of society.

Punishment is seen as an integral aspect of justice to stop people straying from what is good and just.

For many Muslims there are two acts which deserve capital punishment:

- Murder
- Openly attacking and threatening the Muslim way of life, having previously belonged to Islam.

- Two crimes are seen as serious enough for execution: murder and openly attacking Islam
- Surah 17:33 forbids the taking of life 'Nor take life – which Allah has made sacred, except for just cause.'

Islamic law, shariah, is the law of the land in Islamic states. Shariah means 'straight path' and gives both rules and punishments. It is based on the Qur'an and Sunnah. Punishment in Islam is nothing to do with the removal of sin, as only God can forgive, but it is a way of keeping law and order in the country.

Judaism

How do Jews treat people who break laws?
What do Jews teach about capital punishment?

The Torah and Talmud contain many laws giving instruction and guidance about behaviour as well as how crime should be punished.

As Jews believe everyone was given free will people must take responsibility for their actions. Jews see that the aims of punishment include deterrence, protection, retribution and promoting justice. Justice is very important in Judaism. As God created a just world so Jews must practise justice themselves. Deuteronomy 16 states that judges must be appointed who are fair and do not accept bribes.

At Yom Kippur many Jews repent wrongful actions. One of the statements in the Yom Kippur service is 'Repentance, Charity and Devotion can change a grim fate.' Although Jews are taught they should be forgiving, only the victim can forgive. No one can be forgiven on behalf of others.

> 'You shall love your neighbour as yourself.'
> Deuteronomy 17:6

> 'Anyone who commits murder shall be put to death. ... The principle is a life for a life.'
> Leviticus 24:17–18

- Today there are many Jewish views on the issue
- In the Torah, some crimes were punishable by death
- Deuteronomy 17:6 states 'A person shall be put to death only on the testimony of two or more witnesses.
- Leviticus 24:17–18 states 'Anyone who commits murder shall be put to death.'
- In Israel, the death sentence is only used for genocide or treason

Sikhism

How do Sikhs treat people who break laws?
What do Sikhs teach about capital punishment?

For Sikhs there is no distinction between temporal (*miri*) and spiritual (*piri*) power.

At the heart of Sikh belief and practice is the principle of caring – this is not an optional extra, and neither is religion about saving one's own soul. Where things do go wrong, and people do things that they should not, it is because of what Sikh's call haumai. This is ignorance and self-centredness, which result in people not seeing God in others as well as in themselves, and imagining that they are the most important thing around. Once a person realises this it enables them to be supportive and forgiving towards others who make mistakes.

Sikhs believe that for some serious crimes, capital punishment may be necessary, but that it should never be carried out in revenge.

> 'There can be no worship without performing good deeds.'
>
> Adi Granth 4

> 'A place in God's court can only be attained if we do service to others in this world.'
>
> Adi Granth 26

- Wrongdoing is likely to be punished in this life or the next
- Capital punishment is not contrary to the Sikh World View, and may need to be used

Exam Tip

Many candidates lose marks because they do not use technical terms correctly, and do not even give the proper name for the religious traditions they are writing about. Although marks are not taken off for these inaccuracies, it is not possible to gain full marks if they are incorrect.

Task

- Look at the examples of errors below. Can you give the correct terms for each?

Naming religious traditions:	Technical terms:	
'Katholicks'	'reconsilation'	'foregive'
'Prodestants'	'uthenasha'	'fetus'
'Hinduists'	'kishatrias'	'scared'
'Buddhas'	'tempel'	'mosck'
'Sihks'	'sinagoge'	'koran'
'Islams'	'pasifist'	'religios'
'Jewadists'	'sancity'	'inosense'

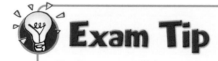 **Exam Tip**

Each topic will have a page of stimulus for you to look at. It is important to spend time looking closely at the picture.

Look at the above picture and answer the following questions

Who – is in the picture?
What – do you think is happening and what do you think is being said to the prisoner?
Where – do you think the picture was taken?
Why – is the prisoner being read to?

From **one** religious tradition, explain what you think the religious believer is saying to the prisoner.

The role of sacred texts

Our authority doesn't just come from the laws of the country. For many religious believers it also comes from their sacred texts and books. Religious believers often consider sacred texts as:

Guidelines – giving guidance on how to live your life. This can often be given through the stories or teachings in the sacred text.
Truth claims – within all sacred texts there are scriptures that are believed to be true and therefore should be followed.
Revelation – at the heart of each religion is the belief that the truth has been given to humanity. It is eternal and for all times. Many people believe that their sacred texts are given by God who reveals the truth to people and so have the authority of God.

Christianity ♱

B **ible** is the name given to the Christian Scriptures. It is made up of two parts, the Old and the New Testaments. Altogether there are 66 different books in the Bible (written in Hebrew and Greek), covering many centuries of life and faith. The Bible has a special place in worship, and many Christians read from it every day.

I **nspired** by God. For some Christians this means it is literally 'the Word of God'; for others, it is believed that God speaks through the Bible, by inspiring Christians as they read and consider its insights and the timeless stories and messages that were written by people inspired by God.

B **asis of faith** – the Bible is the source book of the Christian faith, and it is, particularly in Protestant Churches, seen as the supreme authority in matters of doctrine and belief. This means that it needs to be read, studied and interpreted, by individuals and communities.

L **iving Word** – is the term used by Christians to describe Jesus. They believe him to be 'God made Flesh', and so the clearest way through which God and his will and purpose can be known. This is why the Gospels are so important; they tell of the life and teachings of Jesus, and were written to inspire faith in him.

E **ssential reading** – the Bible has been translated into many different languages, as Christians believe people should read it for themselves and be inspired by it, and try to live according to its teachings and examples.

For me the Bible is a revelation from God and every word is true. I take all the Bible as literally true and the laws and stories act as my authority and guidelines for life.

The Bible is my source of comfort and support. After my grandmother died I gained so much from reading about the sufferings of Jesus and the importance of faith.

Buddhism ☸

P **ali Canon** is the collection of the teachings of the Buddha. It was written down in the language of Pali about 500 years after the life of the Buddha and is mostly used by Theravada Buddhists.

A **nother name** for the Pali Canon is the Tripitaka or Three Baskets – the Vinaya Pitaka, Sutta Pitaka, and Abhidamma Pitaka.

L **aws** or rules that monks and nuns should follow are in the first basket (*Vinya Pitaka*). There is also a section which contains the laws of the Sangha as well as for individual monks. These are kept by the community of monks who recite the 227 rules fortnightly.

I **mportant teachings** of the Buddha are found in the second basket (*Sutta Pitaka*). This also contains the Dhammapada containing the Four Noble Truths and the Noble Eightfold Path. The teachings on meditation are followed by most Buddhists today. The Dhammapada is most likely to be found in a Buddhist's home.

C **hildren enjoy** the Jataka stories found in the Sutta. The stories contain teachings about moral behaviour.

A **bhidhamma Pitaka** is the third basket, and this is a philosophical commentary on the teachings of the Buddha. It is normally only read by the educated monk and the teachings passed on.

N **oble Eightfold Path** is contained in the Sutta Pitaka. These are the eight ways people should live by in order to reach enlightenment.

O **bserving the teachings** of the Pali Canon is essential for all Buddhists. The Buddha insisted that it was his message that was important – not him as a person. Parts of the Canon are often buried in stupas (a small monument building containing sacred relics).

N **uns and monks** will recite selections in the monastery at morning and evening prayers.

> I am a Theravada Buddhist and so the Pali Canon is really important to the way I live. I will often seek guidance on how to live my life by reading the sayings of the Buddha.

Hinduism ॐ

There are many Hindu authoritative texts. One of the best known is 'The Song of the Lord', or Bhagavad Gita.

G **ita** or **Bhagavad Gita** is also known as 'The Song of the Lord', and forms part of the Mahabharata.

I **nspirational**. It is a much loved book and many Hindus can recite at least a part of it. It is told in story form and in plays and films. Gandhi kept a copy of it with him at all times. It is often used for personal study and group recitation. Verses are often recited at a funeral.

T **reated with respect**. It is not placed on the floor nor touched with the feet or dirty hands. Copies are sometimes wrapped in silk cloth.

A **rjuna's conversation** with Krishna is a particularly important teaching text. In his conversation, Krishna advises Arjuna that although he may live or die, the outcome is in the hands of God. He should focus on truth and justice. Many Hindus will consult the dialogue for teachings on *varnashramadharma* (the rules and laws which govern the duties of one's particular caste and stage of life.)

We use our scriptures every day in worship at our home shrine or in the temple. My grandmother has given me comic books and videos of the stories. I am not sure how many of them are really true but I know that the message of each story is really important. It helps me to understand the difference between wrong and right.

Islam ☪

Q **ur'an** is the collection of messages revealed by Allah to the Prophet Muhammad over a period of 23 years. Muslims believe that the Qur'an is speaking the word of Allah.

U **ltimate guidance** for Muslim life. It covers all aspects for all times – unchanging. The message and rules in the Qur'an are for all time. For this reason the Qur'an should be read in Arabic (as it was revealed). Many Muslims become *hafiz* (learn the Qur'an off by heart).

R **espect** is shown by the way the Qur'an is treated. When not in use it should be stored on a high shelf and wrapped in cloth. Before handling it a person should be in a state of wudu and in a suitable frame of mind. When it is being read it will often be placed on a wooden stand.

A **khlaq** (person's attitudes, conduct and ethics) are described in the Qur'an. The Islamic law (*shariah*) comes from the Qur'an and Sunnah as it details whether actions in life are halal or haram and how to live the way that Allah wishes.

N **ations** which have become Islamic States have adopted the shariah law as the law of the country.

For me the Qur'an is a revelation from Allah and is true for all times. It gives me my guidelines on how to pray, what food to eat, how to run a business and how I should behave.

Judaism

T **enakh** is also known as the Written Torah. It consists of the five books of the Law (Torah), the books of the Prophets (*Neviim*) and the holy writings (Ketuvim). The word 'Tenakh' is made up from the first letters of each of the three words.

E **ternal**. The Tenakh is considered as the message for all time as it contains the Torah which is believed to be the Word of God, and contains rules about how Jews should lead their lives. In addition to the Tenakh, the Talmud is also considered very important by many Jews. This contains the Mishnah, or Oral Torah, which are additional teachings given to Moses by God.

N **eviim** is the second part of the Tenakh, and contains stories of the Prophets who were messengers sent to earth by God to teach people, e.g. Isaiah, Amos.

A **uthority**. The Tenakh is used as a source of authority throughout Jewish worship, festivals and daily life. The Sefer Torah in the synagogue is treated with great respect. It is placed in the ark in the Synagogue, and a *yad* (silver pointer) used to read it. If the scroll is damaged, it must not be thrown away but buried with as much respect as if it were a person.

K **etuvim** are the third section of the Tenakh, and although considered holy, they are not seen to be as sacred as the Torah. They contain writings such as Psalms, which may be used in worship, and the stories of Esther and Ruth, which are read at the festivals of Purim and Shavuot.

H **alakah**. This is the collective name referring to the whole of Jewish law as well as to individual laws. It has been built up over the centuries by rabbis to suit modern day issues, e.g. 'Can Jews receive transplant organs from pigs?'. From their considerations, a Responsa is issued. ('Responsa' literally means 'answers'.)

> As an Orthodox Jew I believe that the Torah is the word of God just as it was revealed to Moses. Yes, it was a long time ago but those laws are just as important now as they were then.

> As a reform Jew I think that the Torah was written by people who were inspired by God. I think it reflects the time it was written and so some of the teachings aren't relevant to today and don't need to be followed.

Sikhism

GURU GRANTH

Guru Granth Sahib are the Sikh Scriptures – sometimes known as *Adi Granth*.

Ultimate guide for all Sikhs. After the death of Guru Gobind Singh there were to be no more human gurus, instead all Sikhs would be led by this holy book.

Respect is shown by the way it is treated in the gurdwara. It is not worshipped. When not being read in the gurdwara, it will be covered with three pieces of embroidered cloth, known as rumala.

Uniform. All are written the same in the Gurmukhim script, with 1430 pages and 3384 hymns.

Gurdwaras have the Guru Granth as the place of focus, and there is also a special room where it is 'put to bed' at night.

Read by the Granthi, and whilst it is being read a *chauri* (made of yak's hair fastened to a handle of wood or metal) is waved over the Guru Granth. It is a symbol of authority and power – a reminder to treat the Guru Granth in the same way as royalty.

Akhand paths are continuous or uninterrupted readings of the scriptures, usually used to observe a gurpurb, or festival of the anniversary of a Guru's birthday or death.

Naming ceremony. The Guru Granth is used in the naming ceremony of babies. At a point in the ceremony, the granthi opens the holy book at random, and reads out the first word on the left-hand page. The parents then choose a name for their baby beginning with the first letter of that first word.

Treated like a living guru, or teacher. It is taken each morning and placed on a raised platform (*manji sahib*) with a canopy (*chanani*) in the gurdwara. Worshippers bow before it when entering the room, to show their respect and honour for its place and importance.

Homes only have a copy if they have enough space to have a special room just for the Guru Granth Sahib (often called 'Babaji's Room'). Otherwise they will have a *Gutka*, which contains extracts.

For me as a Sikh the Guru Granth Sahib is the living word. It is our final Guru and is treated with that same respect. There will never be another Guru so the teachings are eternal.

What happens when authorities clash?

Many people have their beliefs or personal convictions that are based upon their views of what is right and wrong. Sometimes these are based upon views of parents, friends, sacred texts and religious teachings but most often from their own conscience.

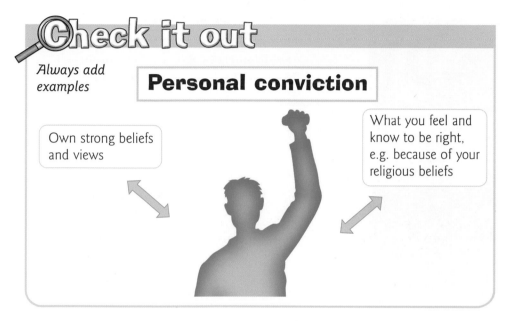

Always add examples

Personal conviction

Own strong beliefs and views

What you feel and know to be right, e.g. because of your religious beliefs

Every week there will be examples in the news where someone's own beliefs clash with another form of authority, such as a school or the law of the land.

> A Christian traffic warden has infuriated his Miami employer by refusing to write traffic tickets as a matter of principle. William Oertwig Jr, 47, hasn't written a ticket in two years and argues that police powers shouldn't be used to collect cash. He has been demoted and is suing Miami-Dade County, claiming the training manual says tickets are given at the officer's discretion. He said, 'I believe that by educating and informing the motorist, I am accomplishing traffic enforcement.'
>
> *Evening Standard*

Task

- For each of the examples on pages 125–26 explain why a conflict exists between personal conviction and authority.

Rosa Parks – bus boycott

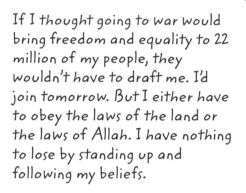

If I thought going to war would bring freedom and equality to 22 million of my people, they wouldn't have to draft me. I'd join tomorrow. But I either have to obey the laws of the land or the laws of Allah. I have nothing to lose by standing up and following my beliefs.

Muhammad Ali – conscientious objector

Protestors against abortion

Muslim woman forced to remove hijab when visiting a prisoner

What if the authority is wrong?

There have been times in history when the secular laws have been wrong. Look at the following images and decide what it was that is now thought wrong, and why.

Suffragette under arrest

Segregation in South Africa (apartheid)

Sometimes, it appears that there may be a clash between sacred and secular laws. Jesus was presented with a dilemma of this sort, by the Pharisees:

'And they came and said to him, "Teacher, we know that you are true, and care for no man; for you do not regard the position of men, but truly teach the way of God. Is it lawful to pay taxes to Caesar, or not? Should we pay them, or should we not?" But knowing their hypocrisy, he said to them, "Why put me to the test? Bring me a coin, and let me look at it." And they brought one. And he said to them, "Whose likeness and inscription is this?" They said to him, "Caesar's". Jesus said to them, "Render to Caesar the things that are Caesar's, and to God the things that are God's." And they were amazed at him.'

Mark 12:13–17

The question put to Jesus was really a trap, for if he had said people should not pay their taxes to Caesar, then the Pharisees would have been able to criticise Jesus for inciting rebellion against their Roman rulers. If Jesus had merely said people should pay Caesar, then they would have been able to criticise him for not bringing God into it at all.

Christians see in this passage a clear reference to Jesus commending his followers to be good citizens; he tells them that if it is a requirement to pay taxes, then they should be paid. But he also makes it clear that when such secular rules do affect us, we should not use that as an excuse for not giving to God what he is due as well.

At other times it is not so clear, and when sacred and secular laws conflict, the individual has to think through their conscience, and make a decision. In these circumstances it may be that a person's conscience will tell them what they ought to do. They will always consider the issues of human rights and ways of seeking justice for others.

Working for human rights

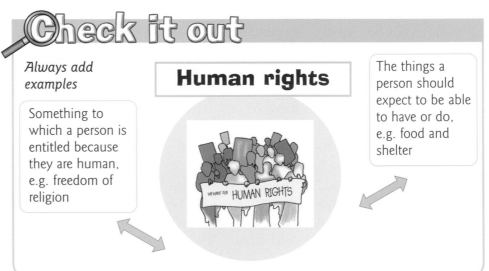

Check it out

Human rights

Always add examples

Something to which a person is entitled because they are human, e.g. freedom of religion

The things a person should expect to be able to have or do, e.g. food and shelter

Task

Often, religious leaders have been in the front line of campaigning for those who do not have the basic human rights, or who face serious discrimination and prejudice. Study the following examples, and consider carefully how their religious convictions led them to do what they did.

Christians believe that all people are equal to God and will use the teachings and actions of Jesus when considering the importance of human rights. Many believe that they should take a stand against unfairness and injustice and will join campaigns in support.

In South Africa, Archbishop Desmond Tutu spoke out against the system of racial discrimination (apartheid). In South America, a Christian movement known as Liberation Theology spoke out against the injustices of the state authority.

'I would like to appeal in a special way to the men of the army, and in particular the troops of the National Guard, the police and the garrison. Brothers, you belong to your own people. You kill your own brother peasants, and in the face of an order to kill that is given by a man, the law of God should prevail that says **do not kill**.'

Oscar Romero

CHRISTIANITY ✟ *OSCAR ROMERO*

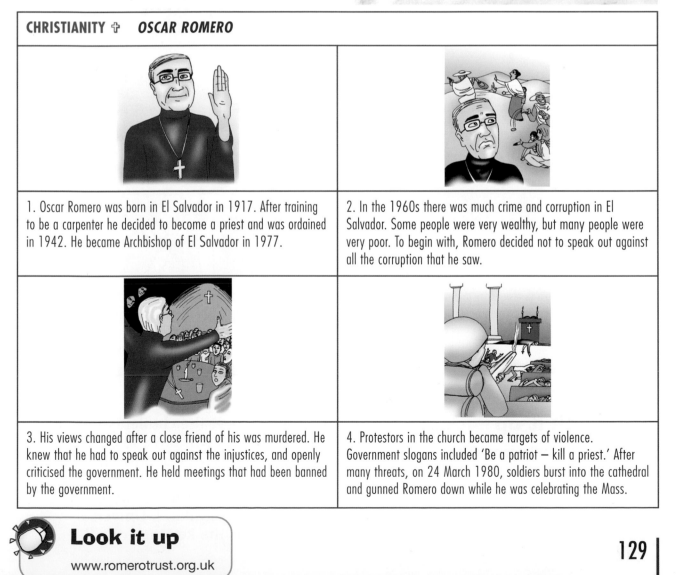

1. Oscar Romero was born in El Salvador in 1917. After training to be a carpenter he decided to become a priest and was ordained in 1942. He became Archbishop of El Salvador in 1977.	2. In the 1960s there was much crime and corruption in El Salvador. Some people were very wealthy, but many people were very poor. To begin with, Romero decided not to speak out against all the corruption that he saw.
3. His views changed after a close friend of his was murdered. He knew that he had to speak out against the injustices, and openly criticised the government. He held meetings that had been banned by the government.	4. Protestors in the church became targets of violence. Government slogans included 'Be a patriot – kill a priest.' After many threats, on 24 March 1980, soldiers burst into the cathedral and gunned Romero down while he was celebrating the Mass.

Look it up

www.romerotrust.org.uk

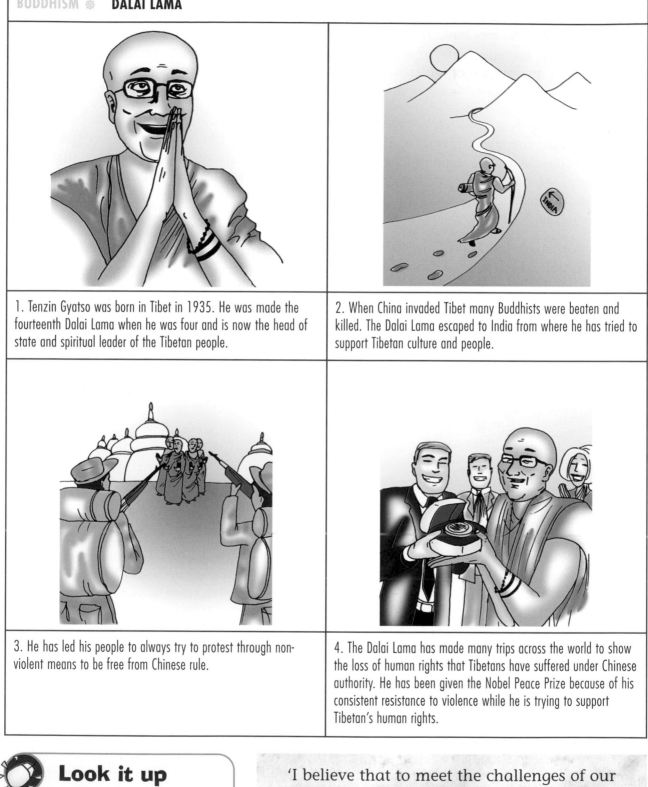

BUDDHISM ❋ **DALAI LAMA**

1. Tenzin Gyatso was born in Tibet in 1935. He was made the fourteenth Dalai Lama when he was four and is now the head of state and spiritual leader of the Tibetan people.

2. When China invaded Tibet many Buddhists were beaten and killed. The Dalai Lama escaped to India from where he has tried to support Tibetan culture and people.

3. He has led his people to always try to protest through non-violent means to be free from Chinese rule.

4. The Dalai Lama has made many trips across the world to show the loss of human rights that Tibetans have suffered under Chinese authority. He has been given the Nobel Peace Prize because of his consistent resistance to violence while he is trying to support Tibetan's human rights.

Look it up

http://www.buddhanet.net

'I believe that to meet the challenges of our times, human beings will have to develop a greater sense of universal responsibility. Each of us must learn to work not just for ourself, one's own family or natural, but for the benefit of all humankind. Universal responsibility is the key to survival.'

Many Hindus have worked to make the world a fairer place. Particular campaigns have been to provide equal opportunities for men and women, to try to gain education for all and to stop the caste system.

HINDUISM ॐ MAHATMA GANDHI

1. Mahatma Gandhi was born in India in 1869, and after studying law in London he returned to India which was governed by British rulers.

2. Gandhi began work in 1894 to use peaceful means to let Indians govern themselves.

3. He used many forms of civil disobedience, including hunger strike, burning of identity passes, and leading a march against the Salt Tax.

4. For all his actions Gandhi always used non-violence as he believed that all life was sacred. He was assassinated in 1948, but even as he lay dying he forgave his killer.

Look it up

www.mkgandhi.org

'You must not lose faith in humanity. Humanity is an ocean; if a few drops of the ocean are dirty, the ocean does not become dirty.'

ISLAM ☾ SHIRIN EBADI

1. Shirin Ebadi was the first female judge in Iran and particularly supported the rights of women and children.

2. In 1979 there was a revolution in Iran. Shirin was forced to resign when it was decided that women were not suitable for such posts as lawyers. Her name was written on death squad's hit lists but Shirin didn't stop supporting people who needed her help. 'When you believe in the righteousness of your path, you take firmer steps. At the same time, being a Muslim and believing in God, I gain more strength as well.'

3. She set up a law practice, taking on cases many Iranian lawyers would not touch, often providing her services at no charge. She was jailed for 25 days in 2000 and spent the time in solitary confinement.

4. In 2003 she became Iran's first Nobel Peace Prize winner. The Nobel committee paid tribute to her courage, noting that she had 'never heeded the threat to her own safety'. The state-sponsored TV channel refused to broadcast Ebadi's acceptance speech because she did not wear the *hijab*, a headscarf that the Iranian government requires all Iranian women to wear, in the awards presentation. Ebadi has long refused to wear the *hijab* outside of Iran. 'Instead of telling Muslim women to cover their heads we should tell them to use their heads,' she remarked.

Look it up

www.writespirit.net/authors/
shirin_ebadi

'It is not Islam at fault, but rather the patriarchal culture that uses its own interpretations to justify whatever it wants.'

JUDAISM ☰ ELIE WIESEL

1. Elie Wiesel was born in Transylvania, which is now part of Romania. When he was fifteen, he and his family were deported by the Nazis to Auschwitz. His mother, father and younger sister perished.

2. After the war Wiesel became a journalist. During an interview he was persuaded to write about his experiences in the death camps.

3. A devoted supporter of Israel, Elie Wiesel has also defended the cause of Soviet Jews, Nicaragua's Miskito Indians, Argentina's Desaparecidos, Cambodian refugees, the Kurds, victims of famine and genocide in Africa, of apartheid sufferers in South Africa, and victims of war in the former Yugoslavia.

4. He is the Chairman of The Elie Wiesel Foundation for Humanity, an organisation he and his wife created to fight indifference, intolerance and injustice. Elie Wiesel has received more than 100 honorary degrees from institutions of higher learning.

 Look it up

www.eliewieselfoundation.org

'And then I explain to him how naïve we were, that the world did know and remained silent. And that is why I swore never to be silent whenever wherever human beings endure suffering and humiliation. We must take sides. Neutrality helps the oppressor, never the victim. Silence encourages the tormentor, never the tormented. Sometimes we must interfere.'

SIKHISM ☬ GURU GOBIND SINGH

1. After the time of Guru Nanak, there had been persecution of many Sikhs and their Gurus. Guru Gobind Singh (1666–1708CE) was the last of the ten living Gurus.

2. He formed a Khalsa (community of the pure) of Sikhs who would be prepared to die for their faith and what they thought was true.

3. The Khalsa fought many battles to defend the Sikh community.

4. Today anyone who agrees to accept the rules governing the Sikh community can receive amrit, and enter the Khalsa.

Look it up

http://www.sikhs.org/guru10.htm

'The greatest comforts and lasting peace are obtained when one eradicates selfishness from within.'

Exam Tip

Sometimes you will be asked for the name and a brief description of the work of an individual or agency.

Always mention specific things done by the person or agency – be brief and concise *and make the comments relevant to the unit.* Someone like Martin Luther King can be an example of a worker for peace (Topic 1), or for human rights (Topic 4), or an example of a conflict between conviction and authority (Topic 1). Always read the question carefully, so that you are clear about the focus for the answer. DO NOT just write all you know about the person or agency!

As a Baptist minister influenced by the teachings of love from Jesus, he:

- used non-violent protests to support civil rights for black Americans
- refused to preach the use of violence and insisted on peaceful and non-violent methods
- staged 'sit-ins' and peaceful 'freedom' marches
- went to jail because of his actions, though no crime had been committed by him
- put into practice the advice of Jesus not to retaliate with violence against harm or injustice, but rather to turn the other cheek, love one's neighbour, and not return hate with hate
- was awarded the Nobel Peace Prize.

Look it up

http://www.thekingcenter.org/about-dr-king

Task

- Using the IMPACT formula (see page 69) construct an outline for two of the individuals in the religious traditions you are studying.
- You may also like to find out about other individuals or organisations that do a similar kind of work in those religious traditions. Local 'non-famous' examples are just as appropriate.

Task

Look at each of the statements below. Decide which you think the religions you are studying would agree with, and explain why.

- If someone killed my best friend I would kill them.
- All human life is sacred.
- The death penalty is no deterrent.
- Life imprisonment is more of a deterrent.
- The victim's family should decide the fate of the murderer.
- Forgiveness is important.
- Everyone bears the image of God.
- We have the responsibility to care for the poor and the powerless.

Task

It is important to build on prior learning. Look back over your work so far, and note down the issues in other topics you have studied in this course that have links with this unit. Issues such as sanctity of life, justice and fairness, reconciliation, etc.

TEST IT OUT

(a) *Explain what religious believers mean by justice.*   [2]

(b) *Explain how having a religious faith might influence a view on human rights.*   [4]

(c) *'There's no point obeying ancient sacred texts.'*
*Give **two** reasons why a religious believer might agree or disagree.*   [4]

(d) *Explain **two** different examples of when there may be a conflict between personal convictions and authority.*   [6]

(e) *'All murderers should be killed.'*
Do you agree? Give reasons or evidence for your answer, showing that you have thought about more than one point of view. You must include reference to religious beliefs in your answer.   [8]

Appendix

Levels of Response Grids for Marking

AO1

2 Mark Questions (question a)

Level	Level Descriptor	Mark total
0	No statement of relevant information or explanation.	0
1	A statement of information or explanation which is limited in scope or content.	1
2	An accurate and appropriate explanation of a central teaching, theme or concept.	2

4 Mark Questions (question b)

Level	Level Descriptor	Mark total
0	Makes no link between beliefs and practices.	0
1	A simple link between beliefs and practices.	1
2	An explicit link between beliefs and practices. Limited use of specialist language.	2
3	Analysis showing some awareness and insight into religious facts, ideas, practices and explanations. Uses and interprets a range of religious language and terms.	3
4	Coherent analysis showing awareness and insight into religious facts, ideas, practices and explanations. Uses religious language and terms extensively and interprets them accurately.	4

6 Mark Questions (question d)

Level	Level Descriptor	Mark total
0	A statement of information or explanation which has no relevant content.	0
1	A relevant statement of information or explanation which is limited in scope.	1
2	An accurate account of information or an appropriate explanation of a central teaching, theme or concept. Limited use of religious language.	2
3	An account or explanation indicating knowledge and understanding of key religious ideas, practices, explanations or concepts. Uses and interprets religious language in appropriate context.	3–4
4	A coherent account or explanation showing awareness and insight into religious facts, ideas, practices and explanations. Uses religious language and terms extensively and interprets them accurately.	5–6

 Appendix

AO2

4 Mark Questions (question c)

Level	Level Descriptor	Mark total
0	Makes no relevant point of view.	0
1	A simple, appropriate justification of a point of view.	1
2	**Either:** An expanded justification of one point of view, with appropriate example and/or illustration, which includes religious teaching. **Or:** Two simple, appropriate justifications of a point of view.	2
3	An expanded justification of one point of view, with appropriate example and/or illustration, which includes religious teaching, with a second simple appropriate justification of a point of view (which may be an alternative to the first).	3
4	An expanded justification of two viewpoints, incorporating the religious teaching and moral aspects at issue and their implications for the individual and the rest of society.	4

8 Mark Questions (question e)

Level	Level Descriptor	Mark total
0	Makes no relevant point of view.	0
1	Communicates clearly and appropriately. **Either:** A simple justification of a point of view, possibly linked to evidence or example and making a simple connection between religion and people's lives. **Or:** Two simple appropriate justifications of points of view.	1–2
2	Communicates clearly and appropriately using limited specialist language. **Either:** An expanded justification of one point of view, with appropriate example which includes religious teaching and/or illustration **AND** either a second simple justification. **Or:** Two appropriate justifications of points of view linked to evidence or example, which includes religious teaching.	3–4
3	Communicates clearly and appropriately using and interpreting specialist language. An expanded justification of one point of view, with appropriate examples which includes religious teaching and/or illustration. There is also an adequate recognition of an alternative or different point of view.	5–6
4	Communicates clearly and appropriately using specialist language extensively and thorough discussion, including alternative or different views of the religious teachings and moral aspects at issue and their implications for the individual and the rest of society. Using relevant evidence and religious or moral reasoning to formulate judgement.	7–8

Index

Entries marked in bold refer to key concepts from the specification

Index